INDIAN ARMS AND ARMOUR

Thom Richardson and
Natasha Bennett

CONTENTS

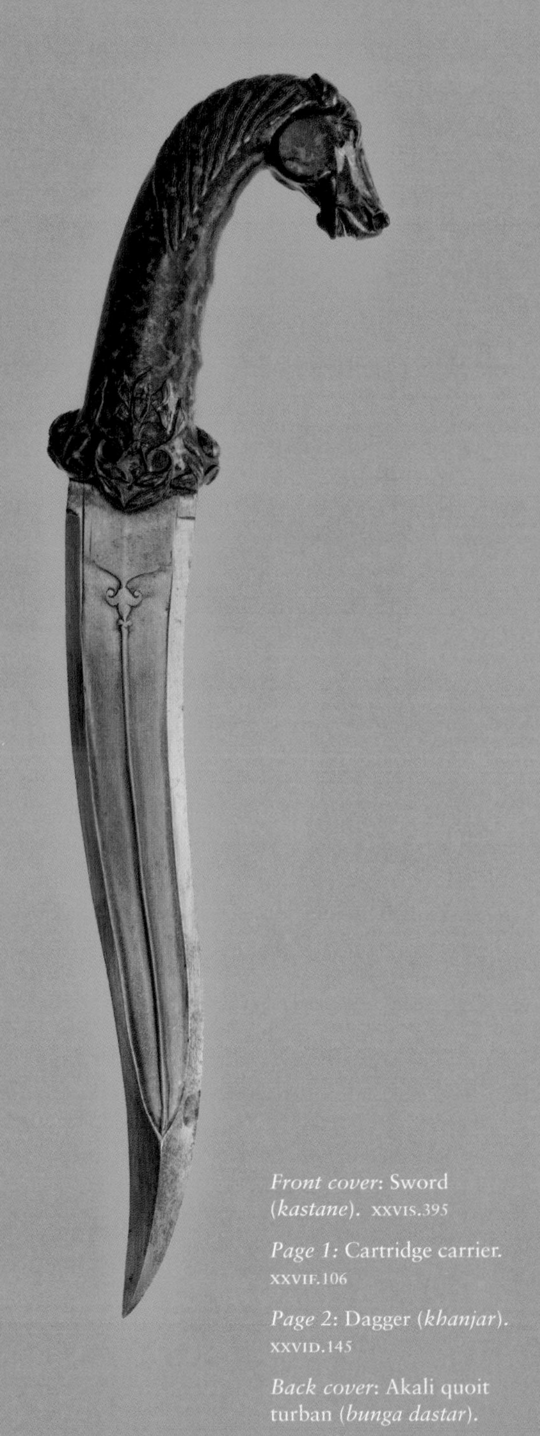

Front cover: Sword (*kastane*). XXVIS.395

Page 1: Cartridge carrier. XXVIF.106

Page 2: Dagger (*khanjar*). XXVID.145

Back cover: Akali quoit turban (*bunga dastar*). XXVIA.60

KASHMIR
PAKISTAN
PANJAB
Lahore
CHINA
UTTAR
SIND
Delhi
NEPAL
RAJASTHAN
Karachi
GUJARAT
Bhopal
MADHYA
PRADESH
BANGLADESH
(BENGAL)
Arabian
Sea
Calcutta
MAHARASHTRA
(DECCAN)
Bombay
ORISSA
Bay of Bengal
Hyderabad
ANDHRA
KARNATAKA
(MYSORE)
SOUTH
INDIA
Mysore
Pondicherry
SRI LANKA
(CELON)
Indian Ocean

2-1896 (9.8) 108/117
۱۲۱

FOREWORD

India is a vast sub-continent, with a complex history and a great array of languages, cultures and religions. This short introduction to one aspect of that great culture is intended merely as an appetiser, and is by no means intended as the last word on any aspect of Indian arms and armour. By 'India' I mean the whole Indian sub-continent rather than any political term. The history which forms a background to the story of Indian arms and armour saw empires rise and fall, but the remarkable constancy in the exquisite weapons used by their defenders and opponents marks Indian arms and armour out as something beyond mere statehood.

Thom Richardson
Deputy Master, Royal Armouries

INTRODUCTION

Though the colonial age of the British Empire in India has come and gone, it was the catalyst to all sorts of studies of Indian culture and it is no accident that much of the pioneering work on Indian arms and armour was carried out by English scholars. The most notable of these, and the author of the first serious study of Indian armour and arms, was William Egerton, Lord Egerton of Tatton in Cheshire, whose catalogue of the collection of the Indian Museum in London (a collection now absorbed into the Victoria and Albert Museum) appeared in 1880. Yet despite a few important works in the 20th century, such as Philip Rawson's *The Indian sword* and Russell Robinson's *Oriental armour*, and new works such as Robert Elgood's *Hindu arms and ritual* in the 21st century, the scientific study of Indian arms and armour has not advanced to the level, say, of Japanese arms and armour.

The scope of this book largely reflects the collections of Indian arms and armour in the Royal Armouries. Almost all the holdings are concentrated in the period from the formation of the Mughal empire in the 16th century to the end of the 19th century when western firearms technology had been widely adopted, and it is hoped that this small publication will help in making an important western collection of Indian armour and arms accessible.

◄ Battle scene from the Akbarnama, about 1590.

ANCIENT ARMS AND ARMOUR IN INDIA

Arms and armour feature as a central part of Indian culture from the earliest times. The heroes of the early epics such as the *Mahabharata* ride on chariots and shoot bows, and archery plays a central role in all Indian military systems up to the widespread introduction of firearms in the 18th century.

Military science

Military science also developed in India, and the military section of the *Arthashastra* of Kautilya, written in the 2nd century BC for the great Maurya king Chandragupta, is one of the most comprehensive descriptions of military equipment and organisation to survive from the ancient world. It describes a fourfold division of arms (infantry, cavalry, chariots and war elephants) that survives to the present embodied in the game of chess, which originated in Sri Lanka in the early centuries AD.

Alexander the Great

The first vivid description of this military system in history is the campaign of the Macedonian army of Alexander the Great against the armies of the Panjab in 325 BC, when Alexander through brilliant generalship defeated the army of King Porus at the battle of the Hydaspes. The threat of even greater Indian armies brought Alexander's campaign of world conquest to an end. The historian Arrian preserves in the *Indike* the account of Nearchus, Alexander's admiral, of the campaign in India. He describes the powerful longbows and long swords of the Indian infantry, and the devastating effect of the numerous war elephants on the Macedonian cavalry that caused the Macedonian army to mutiny against the king who had brought them victorious across the known world. War elephants were such a powerful military force that the successors of Alexander the Great spared no expense in bringing them to the West. Seleukos Nikator, one of Alexander's generals who established a dynasty ruling over present-day Syria, Turkey, Iraq and Iran, and his heirs used large numbers of elephants in their

◄ War elephant from the east gateway of the great Buddhist stupa of Sanchi, 2nd century BC. The mahout sits astride the elephant's neck, while the standard bearers and warriors kneel on the elephant's back. Elephants were used alongside infantry archers and swordsmen in Indian armies from the middle of the 1st millennium BC onwards.

Photo by Karl J Schmidt, Project South Asia, Missouri Southern State University

wars against the other Hellenistic kingdoms and against Rome, while the Ptolemies in Egypt domesticated African forest elephants for military purposes. War chariots drawn by four or even more horses formed the other mounted wing of Indian armies much later than in other parts of Asia, though by the Gupta period (AD 320–550) they had been replaced by armoured cavalry modelled on those of the steppe armies of the Kushans.

Indian chariot

This relief of an ancient Indian chariot is from the scene showing the story of Vessantara on the north gateway of one of the great Buddhist stupas at Sanchi, Madhya Pradesh. Founded by the Maurya Emperor Asoka (273–236 BC), the magnificent gates were added to the sanctuary in the 2nd century BC by the Sunga emperors, and record in detail the arms and armour of the period. Though chariots and carts were used in the Harappan culture, about 3000 BC, it is the Indo-European peoples celebrated in the *Rigveda* who began widely to use war chariots (*ratha*). Drawn by two horses during the Bronze Age, later chariots were drawn by teams of four or more horses, and these continued to be used until the Gupta period (AD 320–550) when they were replaced by armoured cavalry.

▲▼ Details of the north gateway, Sanchi Stupa built in the 2nd century BC.

Photo by Karl J Schmidt, Project South Asia, Missouri Southern State University

North west India

The north west of India has been a magnet for invading armies throughout history. The classical Indian fourfold division was gradually changed by the invaders, for most of the conquerors were cavalry armies, the Saka, Kushans, White Huns, then the Muslim Ghaznavids, Ghurids, Sultans of Delhi and the Mongol Timurids. Those who remained tended to retain their strong cavalry forces and supplement them with war elephants and plentiful Indian infantry.

Dating systems in India

During the medieval and later period a number of different systems of dating were used in the Indian sub-continent. The commonest was the Muslim *hijri* dating, which starts from the flight of the Prophet Muhammad from Mecca to Medina (the *hegira*) on 15 July AD 622. This is a lunar calendar of 12 months, or 354/5 days, so gains a year on the Christian calendar every 33/4 years. A variation on the *hijri* dating, a solar calendar starting from the birth of the Prophet Muhammad in AD 571, called the Mauludi era, was introduced by Tipu Sultan of Mysore. The other main dating found on Indian arms and armour is the Vikrama era, a Hindu calendar which started in 57 BC.

▲ Chiselled decoration on the barrel of a sporting gun made in Seringapatam for Tipu Sultan, dated 1794/5 (1223 AM). XXVIF.46

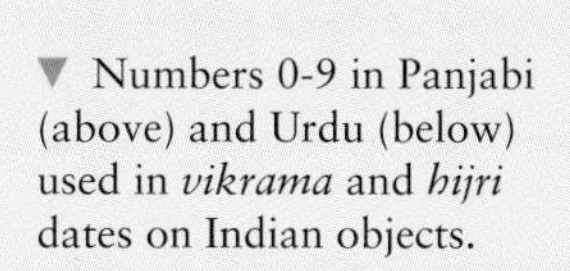

▼ Numbers 0-9 in Panjabi (above) and Urdu (below) used in *vikrama* and *hijri* dates on Indian objects.

੦	੧	੨	੩	੪	੫	੬	੭	੮	੯
۰	۱	۲	۳	۴	۵	۶	۷	۸	۹

THE HILL TRIBES OF CENTRAL AND EASTERN INDIA

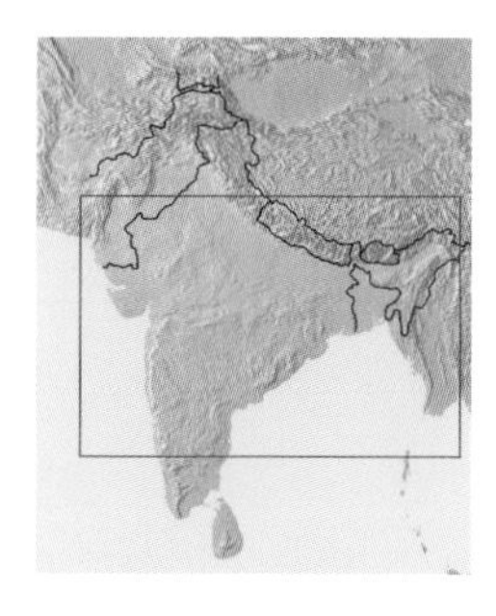

The hills and jungles which separate the Indus-Ganges Plain in the north from the Deccan and the south of India were always a significant barrier to military and political expansion. They prevented all but the most determined invaders from conquering the south of the sub-continent. Armies which ventured into this territory were often lost for months at a time. The impenetrable terrain isolated the many scattered tribal communities from each other and from the outside world. In consequence weapons closely related to those of antiquity survived almost to the present day among these isolated communities.

◄ Khond axe (*tongi*)

Detail of engraving on the blade. XXVIC.22

▼ The hill tribes of Central India.

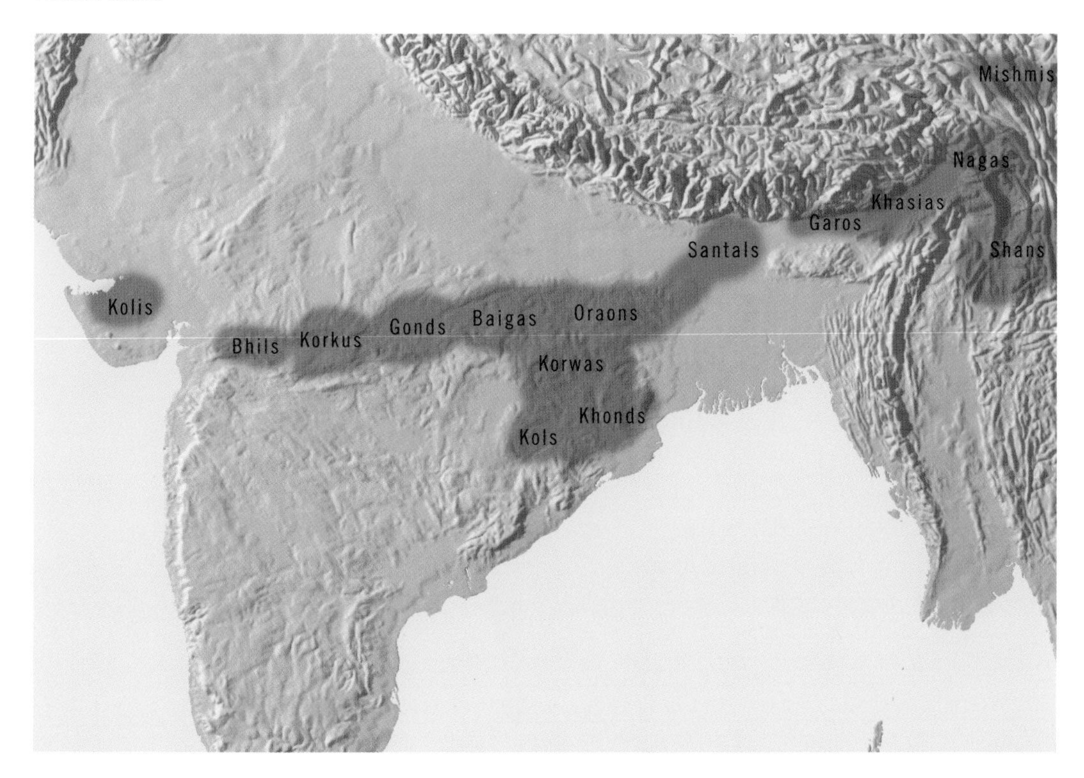

LONGBOW

The old Indian longbow was a self-bow, one made of a single piece of wood. In antiquity it was used throughout India, but was replaced by the more efficient composite bow in the Middle Ages. The old form of Indian longbow survived among the hill tribes of Chota Nagpur, the Mundas, Oraons and Kols. Examples of these in the Royal Armouries collection are self-bows made of bamboo, with raffia strings.

► Self-bow of bamboo (*dhunook*)

From Chota Nagpur. Transferred from the Rotunda Museum of Artillery, Woolwich, 1979, acquired before 1864. XI.150

AXES

The examples of weapons from these areas in the Royal Armouries collection range from those of the Koli people of the far west through the Khonds and inhabitants of Chota Nagpur in the centre, to the Nagas of Nagaland bordering Assam in the east. The western hill tribes of Gujarat, the Kolis, used a distinctive, chisel-bladed form of axe. The principal weapon of the Khond tribes was the two-handed axe. It is distinguished by its wide variety of often multiple-pointed blades. *Tongi* is the Hindi name for them; indigenously, they were called *pharetri*.

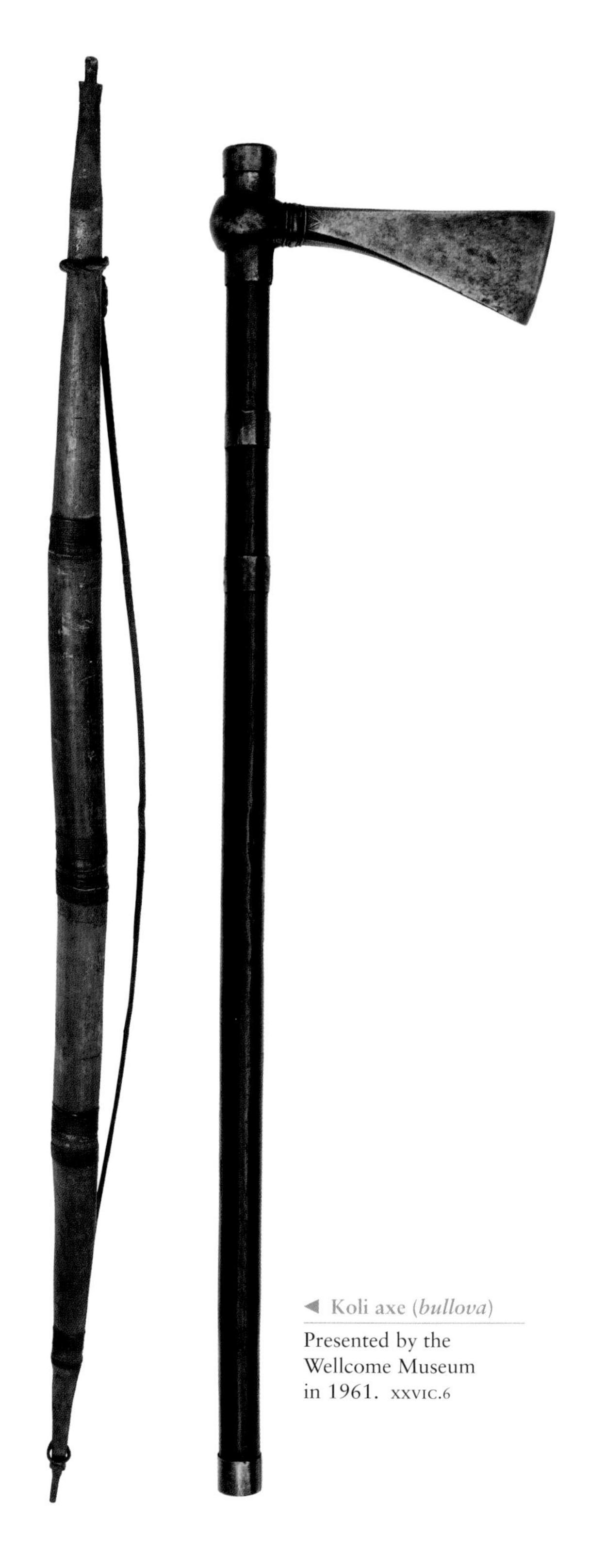

◄ Koli axe (*bullova*)

Presented by the Wellcome Museum in 1961. XXVIC.6

◀ Khond axes (*tongi*)

Four Khond axes acquired in 1859.
XXVIC.20, 22, 24, 23

WEAPONS OF THE NAGAS

A complex of people called the Nagas by their lowland neighbours occupied the hills of Nagaland on the borders of Assam, Burma and India. Males universally carried the *dao*, a broad-bladed, long-handled chopper, worn at the base of the back in a specially designed holder. Throwing spears were primarily used in combat with other villages, as well as in hunting and dances. These were characteristically decorated with tufts of red dyed hair. No armour was worn, but long rectangular shields of hide, wicker or bamboo, often covered with bear or tiger skin, were carried. A rare form of sword, with a stepped blade and tufted cross guard, used by the Angami Nagas in the early 19th century, is preserved in the Royal Armouries collection. Crossbows were also used for hunting.

► Naga spear

Purchased from the Great Exhibition of 1851. XXVIL.168

► Angami Naga sword (*doa*)

Presented by the East India Company in 1851. XXVIS.244

THE NORTH FROM THE MUGHAL CONQUEST TO THE BRITISH RAJ

The Mughals were the most successful Muslim conquerors of India. The founder of the Mughal dynasty, Babur, was a Mongol, descended from Timur and Genghis Khan. He established a foothold in India in the 1520s, and his son Humayun re-established control over Delhi in 1555. But it was Humayun's son Akbar (1556–1605) who built an empire which dominated the north of India. The empire reached its greatest extent under Aurangzeb Almagir (Earth Shaker) (1658–1707), but declined until the last Mughal emperor was deposed by the British for his complicity in the Indian Sepoy Mutiny of 1857.

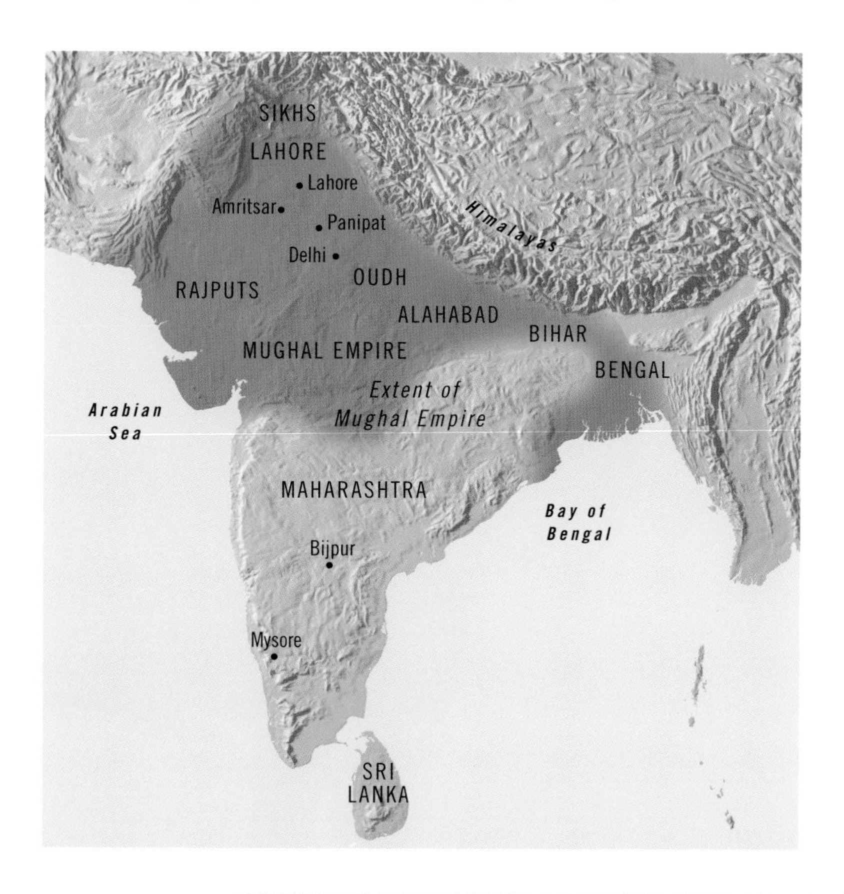

► The extent of the Mughal Empire under Akbar (1556-1605).

MUGHAL WEAPONS

The Mughals were the successors of the Timurids and their armies reflected their Mongol inheritance. They continued to use light cavalry, but became predominantly a heavy cavalry army composed of Turks, Afghans, Persians, and Hindus. Their principal weapons were the composite bow, sword, and spear. The heavy cavalry wore mail and plate armour (*zereh bagtar*) with helmets (*kolah zereh*), and their horses were also protected by armour (*bargustavan*). The weapons they carried were the sword, composite bow, lance, mace (*gorz*) and the saddle axe (*tabarzin*), and a shield (*dhal*) was also carried. The main advantage the Mughal armies had over their contemporaries in India however was in firearms. The extensive use of gunpowder artillery in sieges enabled the Mughals to subdue the hill fortresses of Rajasthan. They also pioneered the use of artillery on the battlefield, in combination with infantry armed with matchlock muskets. It was these arms that brought about the victory over the Sultans of Delhi at the battle of Panipat in 1526.

▼ Mail and plate armour for man and horse (*zereh bagtar* and *bargustavan*), Mughal, about 1600. The shield, bowcase, bow and arrows are modern replicas. XXVIA.203, 258, XXVIH.18

ARCHERY

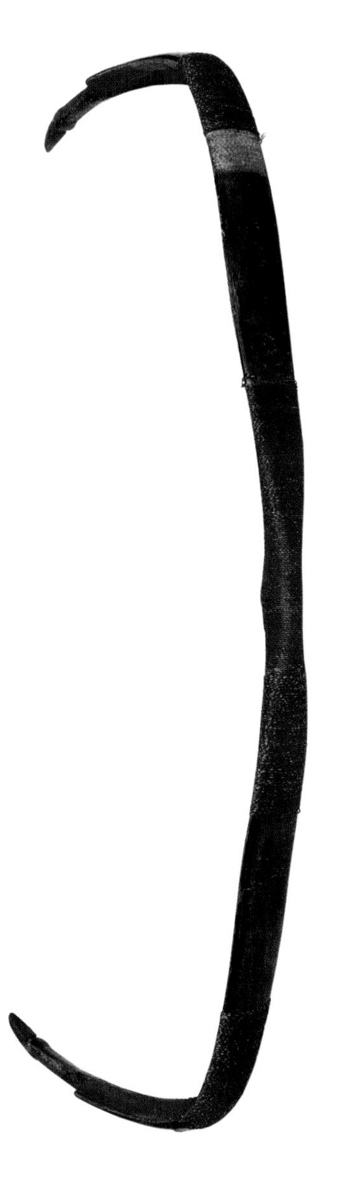

The composite bow (*kaman*) was the characteristic missile weapon of both Indian cavalry and infantry before the 18th century. They are called composite bows because they were made from a combination of different materials, horn, wood and sinew, glued together. The horn, which is very springy under compression, formed the belly of the bow (the side held towards the shooter). The sinew is very elastic when stretched, and formed the back of the bow. A wooden core served as a base for the other materials, and also formed the grip and the rigid 'ears' of the bow, into which were cut the nocks for the bow-strings. The combination of materials made them very powerful despite their short length, which in turn enabled them to be used easily from horseback. Bows of this type are also 'recurved', that is, they bend in their relaxed state in the opposite direction to the curve they hold when they are strung.

◀ Composite bow (*kaman*)

From Gwalior in eastern Rajasthan, presented by the East India Company in 1851.
XXVIB.8

▶ Materials of a composite bow.

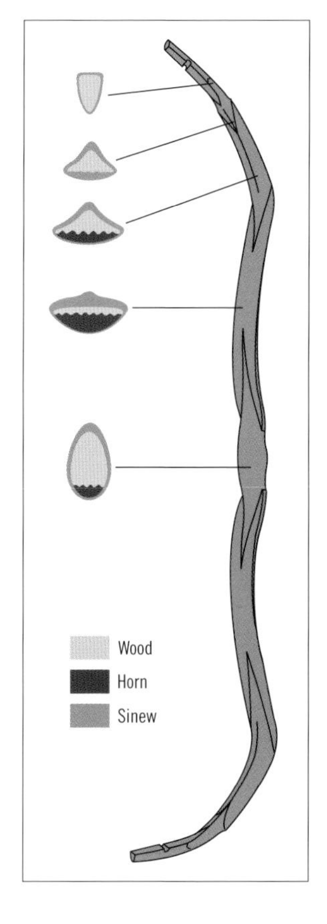

THUMB RINGS

Bows were shot using a thumb release (rather than the finger release or Mediterranean release practised in most European archery). For this release a thumb ring (*zehgir* or *shast*) was used. The Mughal thumb ring was shaped with a characteristic extension to one side. The bow string was held under tension by the ring and a small movement of the thumb released the string, shooting the arrow forward. Because of the thumb release the arrow was shot from the right side of the bow, rather than from the left side as it was in western archery. Archers' rings were made from stone, metal, ivory or bone. They were often decorated with gold, silver, and precious or semi-precious stones. The bowstrings (*zel*) were made of silk or of gut bound with silk.

Detail of battle scene from the Akbarnama, about 1590. © Victoria and Albert Museum, London

▼ Bowstring (*zel*)

Made of green silk, presented by the East India Company in 1851. XXVIB.103

▶ Mughal thumb ring (*shast*)

Made of jade, of the 18th century. XXVIB.46

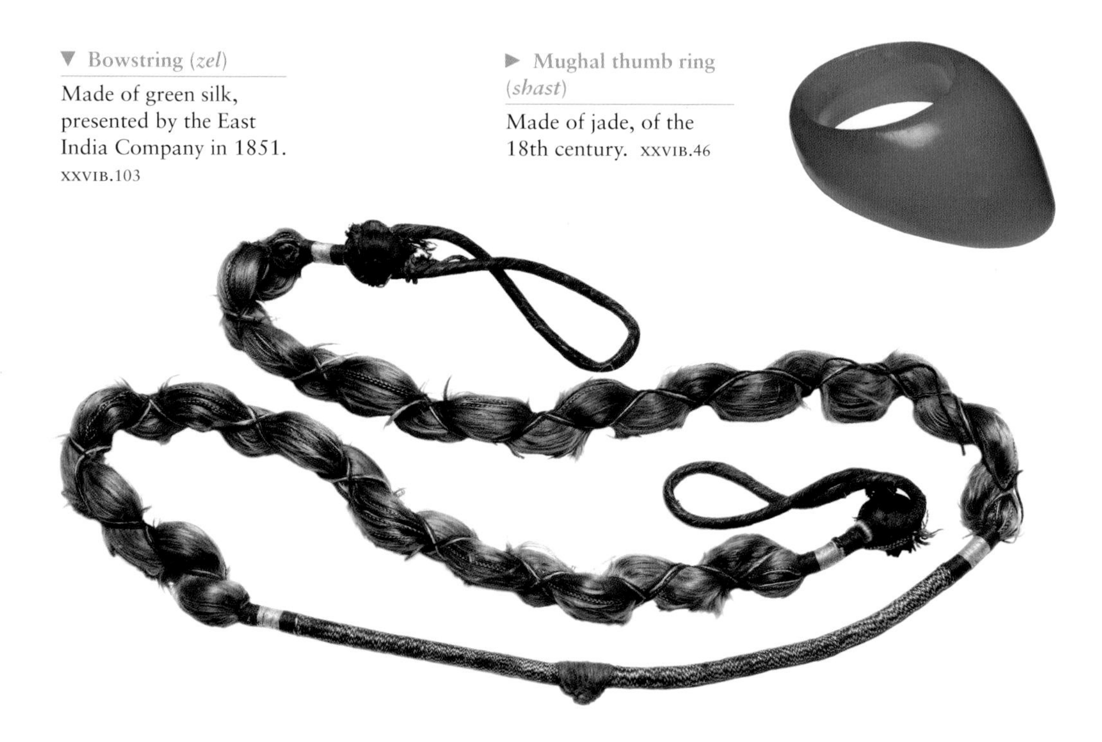

ARROWS

This hunting arrowhead has sloping shoulders carved as leaves and a spear point. Traces of gilding still remain on the head. Artistry and workmanship of the best quality were applied even to such small items.

◀ Quiver and arrows

From Gwalior in eastern Rajasthan, presented by the East India Company in 1851. XXVIB.32

◀ Mughal arrow-head

Fretted Mughal arrow-head of the 17th century. XXVIB.69

SWORDS

TALWAR

With the introduction of central Asian cavalry warfare into India from the 13th century onward, the Asian curved blade sword became the preferred type throughout much of India. Called *shamshir* in Persia, *pulouar* in Afghanistan, the local name for them in India was *talwar*. They developed a distinctive north Indian form of hilt with a disc pommel, itself with regional variations, though the Persian form of hilt with a pistol grip was popular in some areas such as Sind and Lucknow. Another curved sword, this time with a forward-curved blade, was the *sosun pata*.

◄ Curved sword (*talwar*)

With a hilt decorated in fine gold koftgari with garden scenes, Mughal, 17th century. AL.290.60

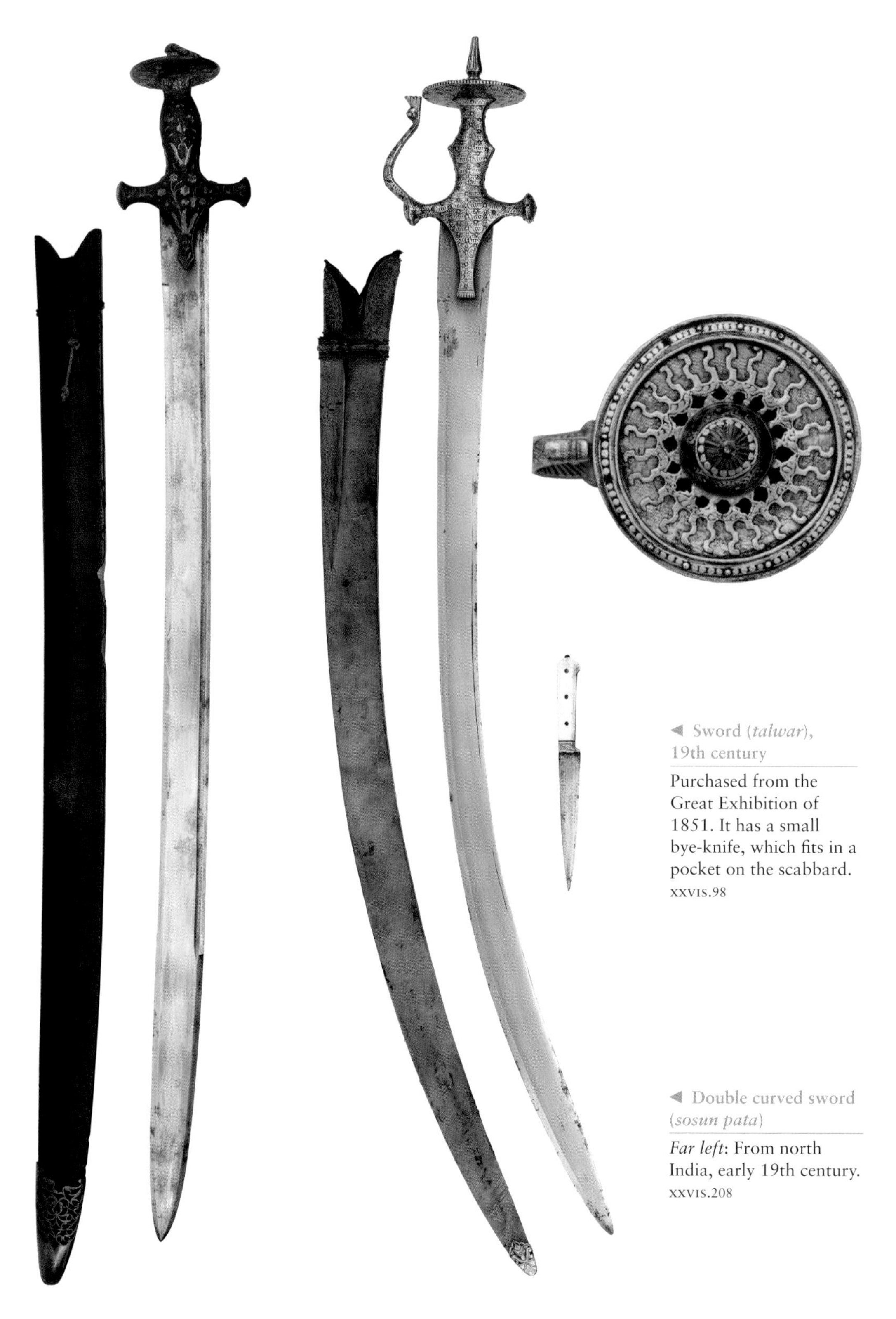

◀ Sword (*talwar*), 19th century

Purchased from the Great Exhibition of 1851. It has a small bye-knife, which fits in a pocket on the scabbard.
XXVIS.98

◀ Double curved sword (*sosun pata*)

Far left: From north India, early 19th century.
XXVIS.208

KHANDA

The indigenous Indian sword had a straight, double-edged blade, and this survived into the post-medieval period as the *khanda*, usually with a basket hilt with a solid guard protecting the hand.

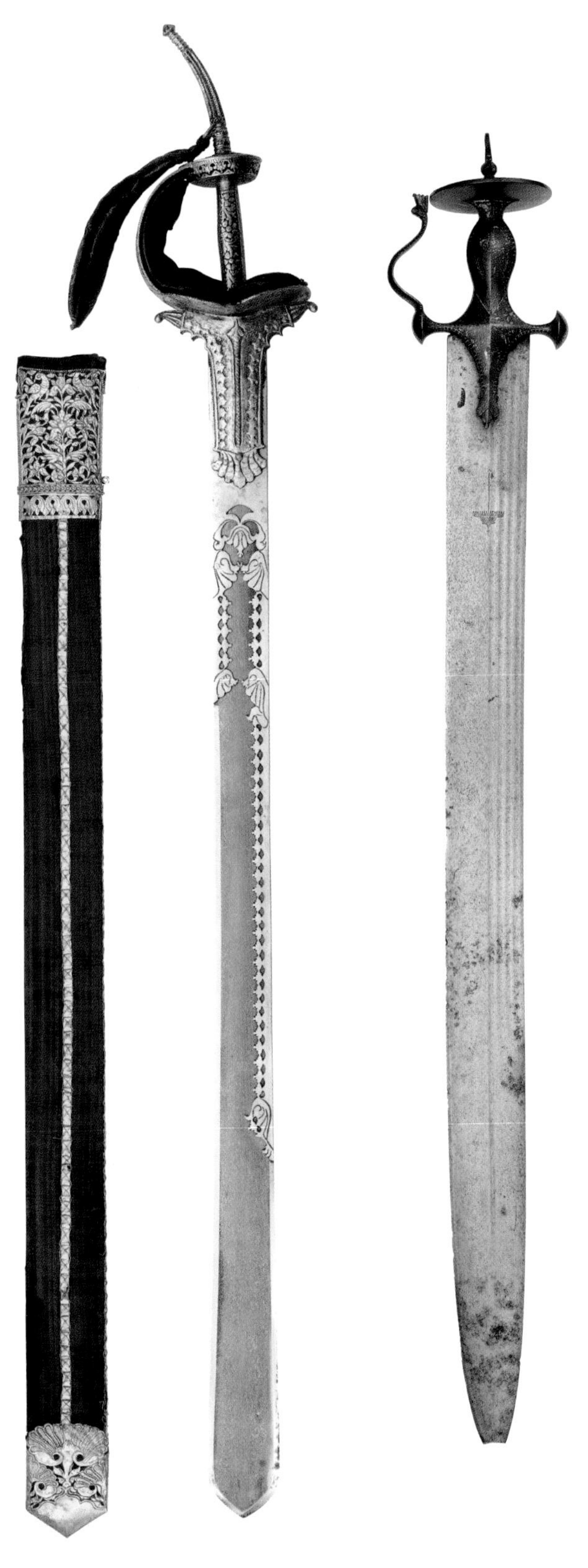

▲► Straight sword (*khanda*) and scabbard,

From Rajasthan, early 19th century. From the Great Exhibition of 1851.
XXVIS.81

► Mughal straight sword (*khanda*)

Far right: Dated 1632–3, from the Indian Disarmament of 1859.
XXVIS.25

PATA

Another form of sword associated more with central India than with the north, but also most commonly fitted with an imported blade is the gauntlet sword or *pata*. This, like the punch dagger or *katar*, has a transverse grip, in this case held inside a steel gauntlet protecting the outside of the hand and forearm.

► Gauntlet sword (*pata*)

Far right: From central India, 18th century with a European blade. XXVIS.182

FIRANGHI

From the early 17th century a fashion for carrying swords with European rapier or broadsword blades, usually with old Indian basket hilts, grew up, and these swords were commonly called *firanghi*.

► Sword (*firanghi*)

With an Indian basket hilt and a European broadsword blade and scabbard, 18th century from central India. XXVIS.83

SHIELDS

The vast majority of medieval and later shields from India are of the same form, circular, slightly convex, and fitted with a central grip formed of two hand loops. These are held by four robust iron loops which are riveted through the shield and secured by large bosses on the exterior. The two grips are held together in the left hand, rather than having the arm passed through them, so the shield can be moved around to block blows and missiles dextrously and rapidly. A fabric suspension loop was often attached to two of the loops so the shield could be slung over the shoulder when not in use. Most shields were of leather, either of buffalo hide or rhinoceros hide, or of steel.

► Shield (*dhal*)

Made in Lahore about 1830–45, showing the lined interior with the central pad and the two hand grips retained by the loops on the inside of the four bosses.
XXVIA.237

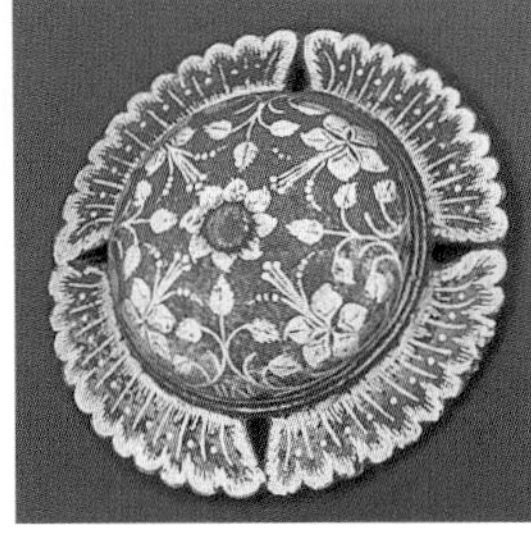

Detail showing one of the decorated bosses.

▲ Mughal shield

Made of buffalo hide, with steel bosses and decorative crescent overlaid with gold, dated 1767/8 (1118AH). AL.290.107

Royal Collection Trust/© Her Majesty Queen Elizabeth II 2015

► Infantryman with shield and spear from the border of the portrait of Rustam Khan, c.1650-58, from the Late Shah Jahan Album. CBL In 07B.35

© The Trustees of the Chester Beatty Library, Dublin

Pistol shield

A leather *dhal* fitted with percussion guns in the bosses. The four pistols built into this shield were discharged two at a time through the bosses on the front of the shield, the muzzle covers were lifted manually first. The percussion mechanism was mounted inside the shield where the knuckle pad would normally be and was fired by means of two triggers. The shield was made in the arsenal of the Rajah of Kola. Rajasthan, mid 19th century, purchased in the Great Exhibition of 1851. XXVIA.83

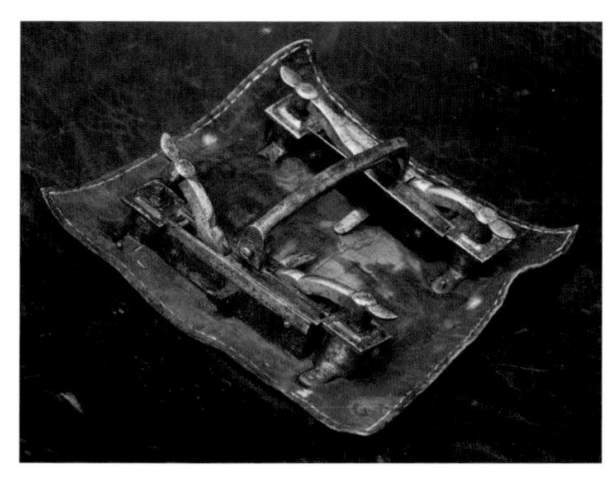

The percussion mechanism.

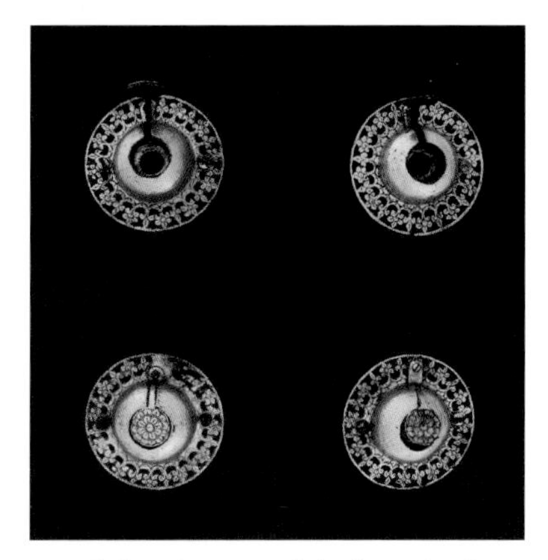

Detail showing two of the four pistols.

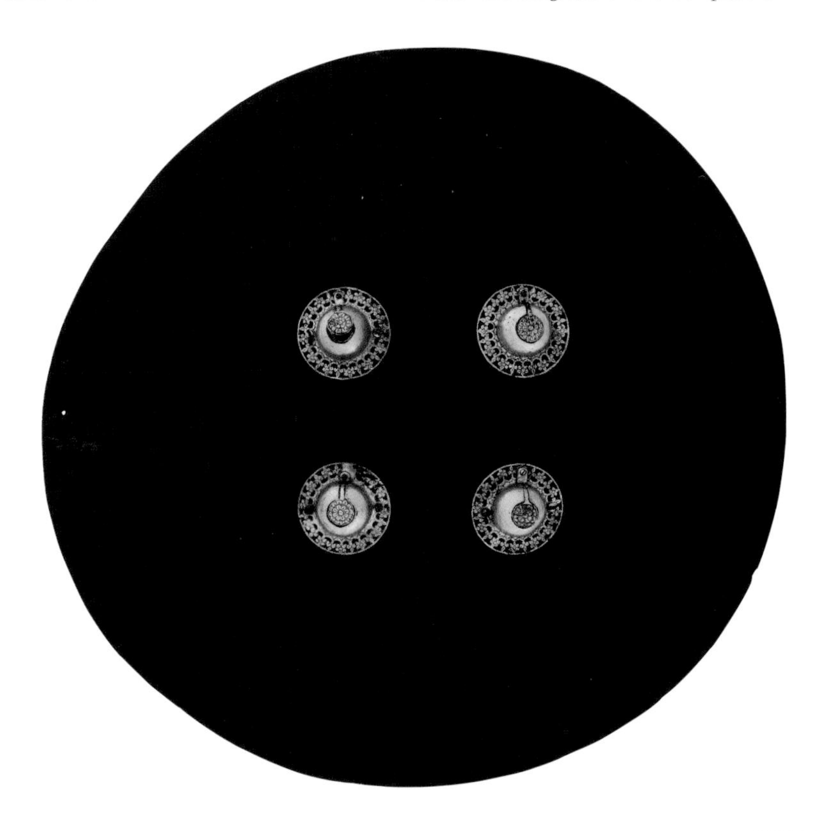

DAGGERS

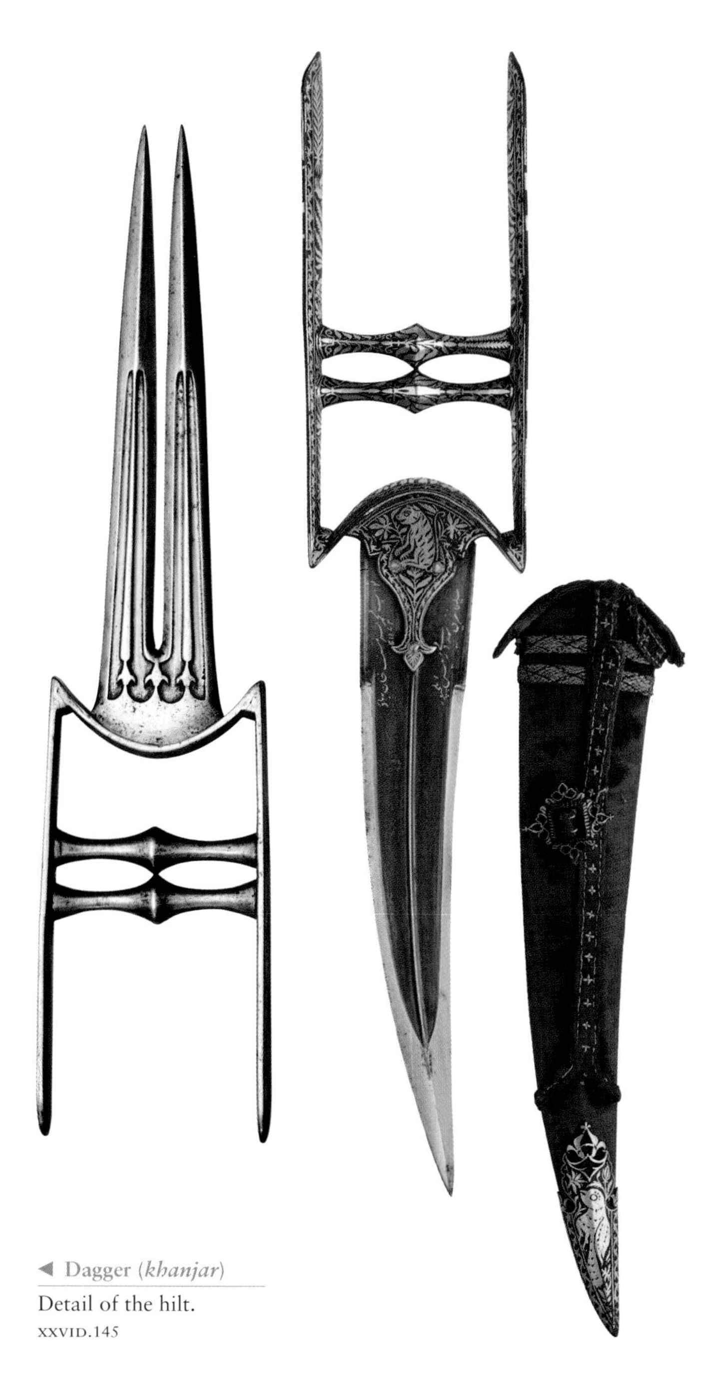

◀ Dagger (*khanjar*)

Detail of the hilt. XXVID.145

KATAR

The *katar*, with its transverse grip, was unique to India, and was to be found across most of the sub-continent. It was fitted with a wide variety of blades, ranging from narrow wavy blades preferred in the south to short, straight and broad blades in the north, multiple blades, as well as novelties such as the 'scissors' *katar*, in which squeezing the grips together causes an outer set of blades to open like scissors, and even multiple daggers in which one or even two little *katar* were housed inside the outer dagger.

◀ Double-bladed punch dagger (*katar*)

Left: From Rajasthan, 18th century, with slightly reinforced points on the straight blades. XXVID.70

◀ Punch dagger (*katar*)

Northern India. With a curved blade inscribed in gold inlay 'Nawab Muhammad Samast Khan Bahadur, 1173 AH [AD 1759–60], may you live like Solomon'. XXVID.146

KHANJAR

The *khanjar* is the commonest type of dagger, found in a variety of forms across the Muslim world. It has a double-edged and double curved blade, and in India often has a reinforced point to give strength to enable the blade to be used against mail armour. Rock crystal, nephrite (jade) and other hardstones usually form the hilts of these daggers, and they are often carved in the form of animal's heads, and set with precious and semi-precious stones in gold. Daggers such as this are often seen in portraits of Mughal nobles.

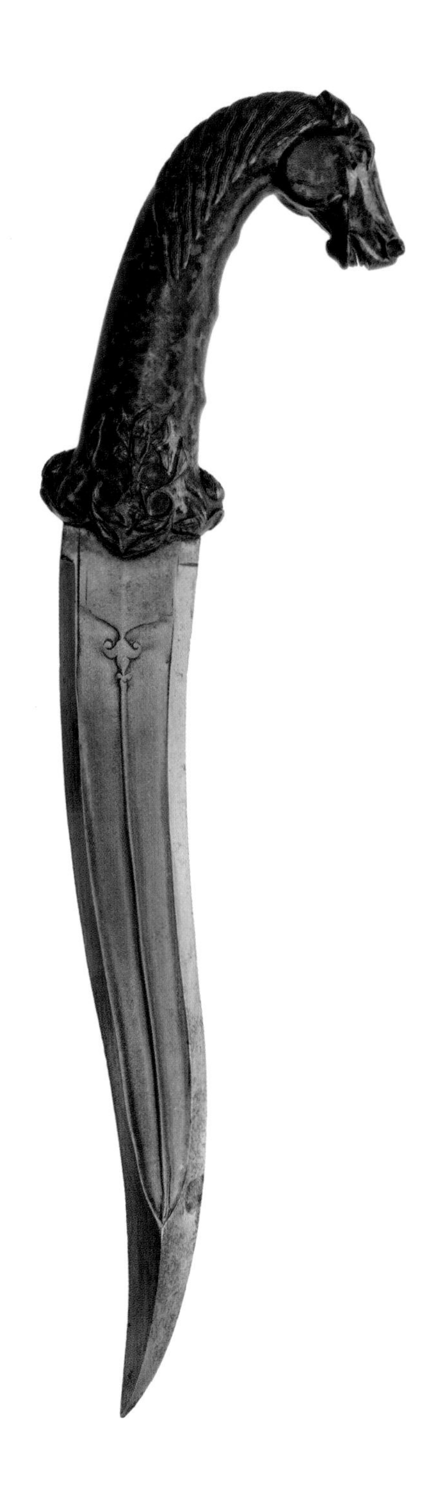

▶ Dagger (*khanjar*)

The hilt is of serpentine carved in the form of a horse's head, Mughal, late 17th century. XXVID.145

PUSHQABZ

Found only in the north was the *pushqabz*, a dagger with a single-edged blade, either straight or double-curved, with a T-shaped back and a long taper to the point, which was sometimes reinforced. It is closely related to the larger and usually straight-bladed Afghan 'Khyber knife' or *chura*. A smaller version, called the *kard*, had a single-edged, flat-backed straight blade. Both had deep scabbards which conceal most of the hilt of the dagger (giving the *pushqabz* its name, 'hidden hilt').

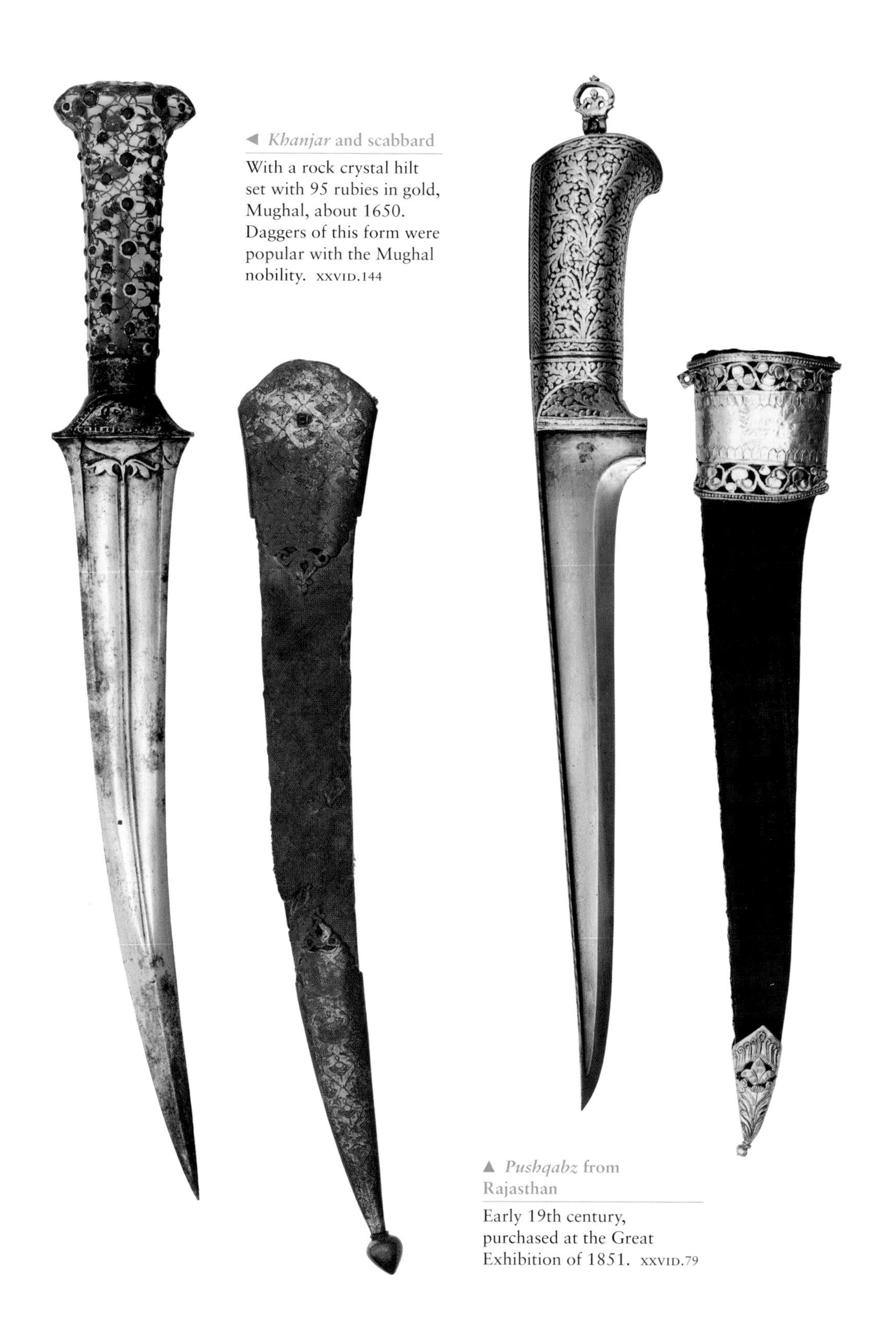

◀ *Khanjar* and scabbard

With a rock crystal hilt set with 95 rubies in gold, Mughal, about 1650. Daggers of this form were popular with the Mughal nobility. XXVID.144

▲ *Pushqabz* from Rajasthan

Early 19th century, purchased at the Great Exhibition of 1851. XXVID.79

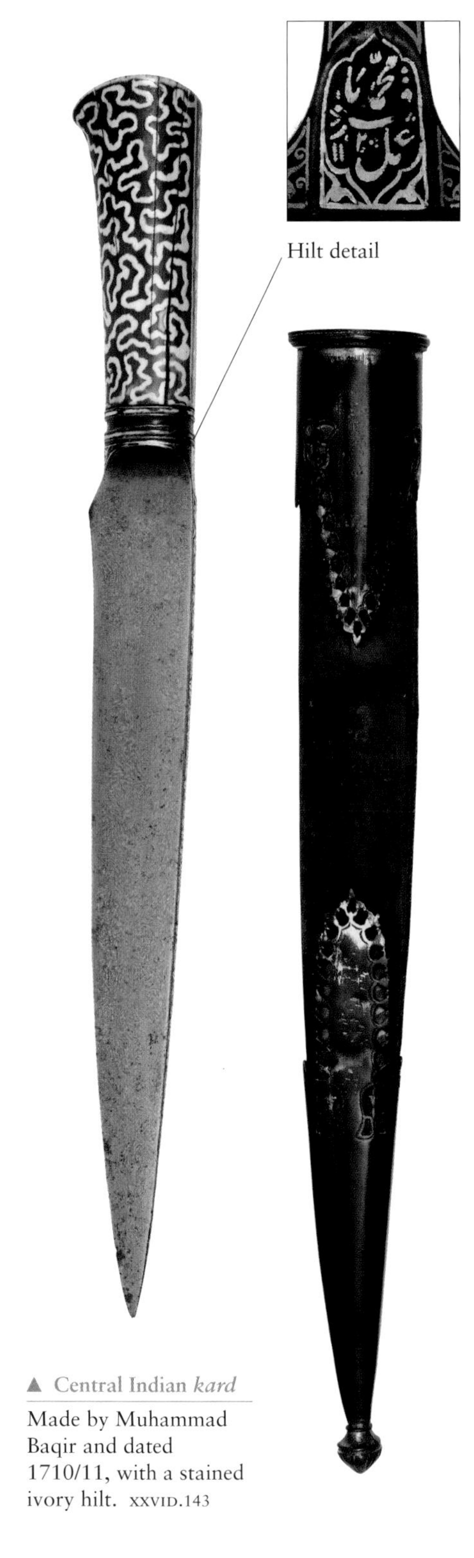

▲ Central Indian *kard*

Made by Muhammad Baqir and dated 1710/11, with a stained ivory hilt. XXVID.143

Steel

From the early centuries AD the Indian sub-continent was an important source of high quality steel, which was particularly important for weapon making. The traditional centre of manufacture was south India and Sri Lanka, and the steel they made was called in the West *wootz*, a corruption of a Telugu-Kannada word for steel. Ingots of steel were made in sealed crucibles, by combining wrought iron with carbon from wood in a reducing atmosphere which caused the carbon to alloy with the iron. This produced a super high carbon steel of considerable strength and sharpness, which also had a very beautiful watered pattern in the metal itself, caused by the dispersion of cementite particles in the pearlite structure of the steel. This watered crucible steel is today sometimes called 'Damascus' steel, incorrectly as it was never made there.

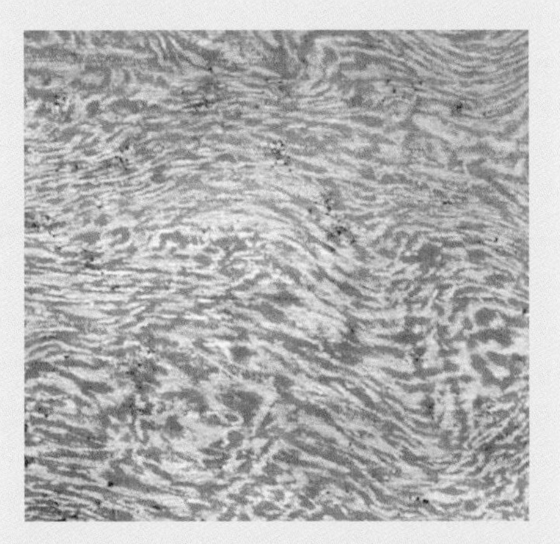

Close up showing watered steel. XXVID.143

OTHER HAND-TO-HAND WEAPONS

► Mace (*gorz*)

Probably Sikh, from Lahore, 18th century.
XXVIC.37

► Spear with butt spike

Far right:
The shaft is of bamboo covered with a painted scene cotaining figures and animals. Indian, 18th century.
XXVIL.221

MACE

The mace (*gorz*) was used extensively in northern India. Not only did it have a symbolism of office and chivalry among the Turks, but it was also an effective combat weapon against an armoured foe, so became a favourite weapon for cavalry combats. Most Indian maces are therefore quite short and designed to be wielded in one hand. Some are fitted with sword hilts, mostly of the old Indian basket variety.

SPEARS

Spears (*nezah*) were also used by cavalry in close combat. Indian cavalry were famed for their skill in duelling with spears on horseback, and examples in the Royal Armouries collection are made of tapering bamboo, with small heads and relatively large butt spikes, so they balance very close indeed to the butt (and have a velvet grip at that point for the purpose). Because the bamboo is hollow, the spear is very light in weight for its size.

Another form of spear found all over northern India is the *barcha*, a spear made totally of steel, used by infantry rather than cavalry, but much lighter in weight than one might imagine. Another spear usually used by foot soldiers is the *ballam*, a short broad-headed spear. The same word was used in *pandi ballam*, the pig-sticking spear beloved of the British Raj in India.

FLAIL

Short flails, with spiked balls attached to the shaft by chain, were also made as hand-to-hand weapons in north India (these are often depicted as medieval European weapons, but they originated in the East).

► Flail, Sikh

Probably from Lahore, late 19th century. XXVIC.45

SADDLE AXE

The saddle axe (*tabarzin*) had exactly the same combat benefits, and was used by armoured cavalry as an alternative to the mace. Again these are short weapons intended for single-handed use.

► Saddle axe (tabarzin)

Probably Sikh, from Lahore, 18th century. XXVIC.33

CONCEALED WEAPONS

Two concealed weapons closely associated with the Mahrattas are the *bagh nakh* and the *bichwa*. The *bagh nakh* or tiger-claw is a set of steel claws mounted on a bar with a loop at either end for the index and little fingers. The *bichwa*, or scorpion, is a short-bladed dagger with a loop grip for the fingers. The principal claim to fame of these weapons is that both were used by the famous leader Sivaji, who ruled Maharashtra in Western India during the 17th century, to assassinate the Bijapur general Afzal Khan, an envoy of the Mughal emperor Aurangzeb.

◄ Tiger claw (*bagh nakh*)

Lashkar near Gwalior, 18th century. Presented by the East India Company, 1851. XXVIM.11

▲ 'Scorpion' dagger (*bichwa*)

Mysore, late 18th century. Acquired before 1859. XXVID.54

Decoration

One of the most distinctive features of arms and armour from all over India was the way in which even quite functional weapons were often highly decorated. On iron and steel this decoration was most often carried out using a technique called *koftgari*, a method of inlaying gold and silver. In fact the technique is most properly called overlay. It was done by cross-hatching the surface with a file, then hammering the gold or silver wire into the hatched surface. The technique is also found throughout the Islamic world, and is sometimes called 'false damascening' (as contrasted with 'true' damascening, in which gold or silver wire was hammered into chiselled channels, a far more time-consuming process). Neither technique had any particular connection with the city of Damascus, though both were carried on there.

ARMOUR

SCALE

The earliest forms of armour from India are of scale. Rare examples of these are found in the post-medieval period, including one armour made of scales of the pangolin (scaly anteater). This was made in Bengal, probably in the early 19th century. The scales have been decorated in gold and the larger scales have been used where more protection is required. It was presented to King George III by Francis Rawdon, Governor of Bengal 1812–22, in 1820.

▼ Scale armour

Made of the scales of the scaly anteater or pangolin in Bengal, probably in the early 19th century. AL.290.13

◀ Detail from a 19th-century helmet decorated with European symbols. XXVIA.12

MAIL AND PLATE

Mail armour was probably introduced into India by the Arabs in the 8th century. The form of mail made with alternate rows of riveted and solid links became characteristic of Indian mail, and survived until the 18th century.

Contact with central Asia brought in a form of fabric armour, quilted and studded with rivets, called the *chihal'ta hazar masha* (coat of a thousand nails). These textile armours often incorporated metal plates to reinforce areas of the body which required greater protection.

▲ Armour (*chihal'ta hazar masha*)

Indian, Mughal, 18th century. XXVIA.197

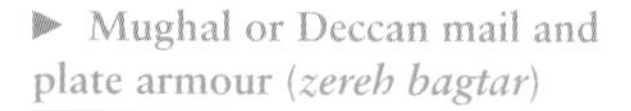

► Mughal or Deccan mail and plate armour (*zereh bagtar*)

Probably 16th century. From the armoury of Bikanir in Rajasthan, this forms part of the spoils of the siege of Adoni in the Deccan in 1682. XXVIA.296

▼ Detail of the mail on the same armour showing the alternate rows of riveted and solid links, and the round-headed rivets of the riveted links. XXVIA.296

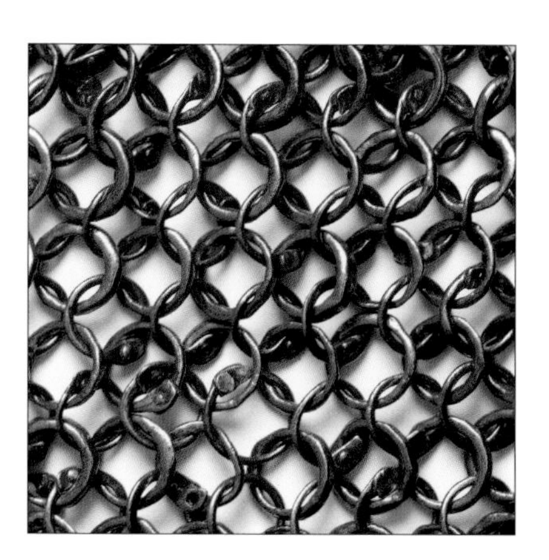

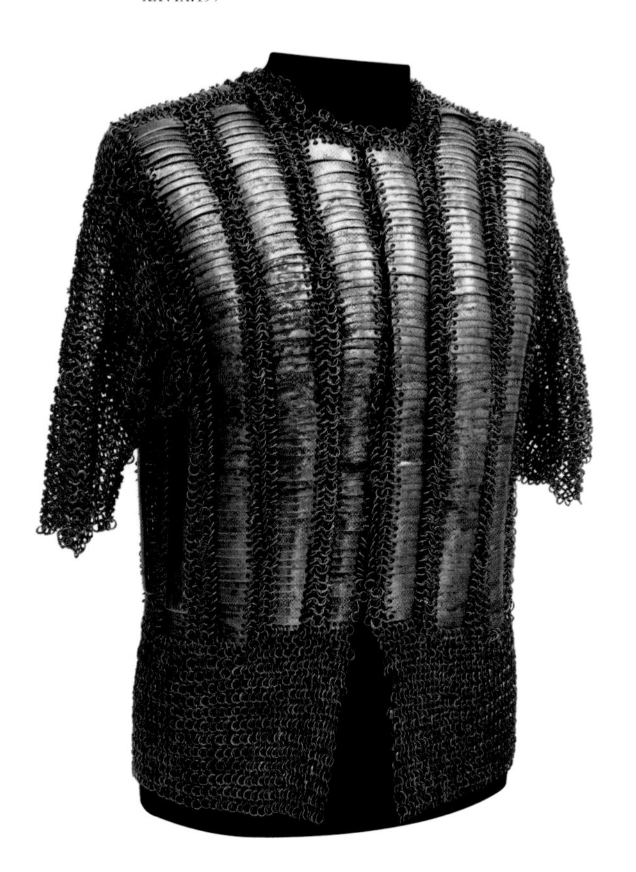

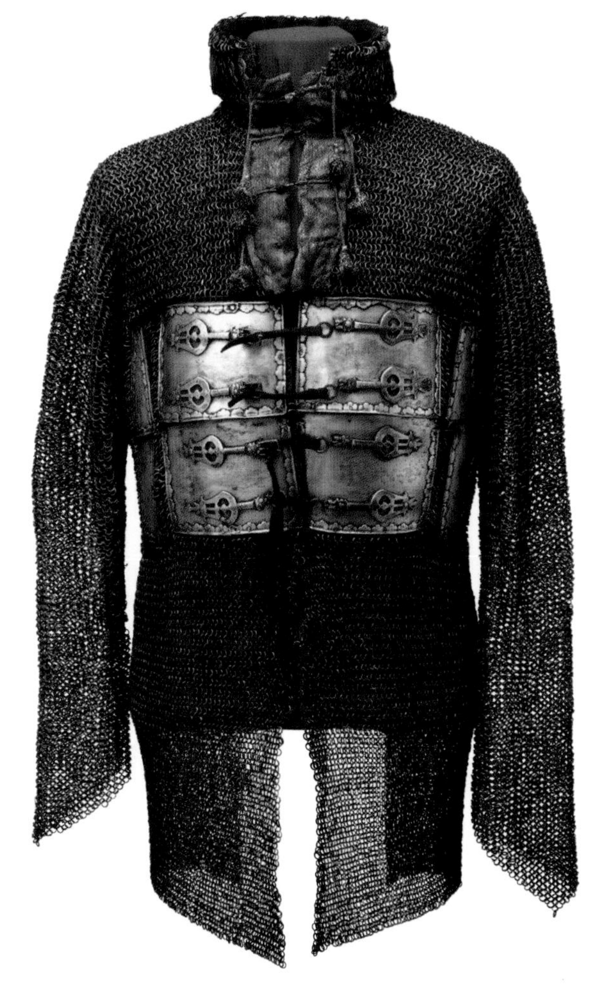

Mail and plate armour was probably introduced into India under the Mughals. It became the standard type of defence, and continued to be used until the 18th century. The coat (*zereh bagtar*), and helmet (*kolah zereh*) are constructed from small overlapping iron scales of various sizes which are connected by rows of mail links. The Mughal coats are distinguished from those of the Near East by the large plates at the front, though some Mughal coats preserved in Rajasthan and either made there or in the Deccan have rows of small scales at the back and front. Trousers of mail (*pajama zirah*) were worn on the legs. All this armour was originally fitted with quilted linings, which rarely survive. The forearms and hands were protected by plate vambraces, called *dastana* or *bazuband*. From the 16th century these were made of two plates joined together with hinges on the outside of the arm and with straps on the inside, extending over the point of the elbow and comfortably padded inside, with mitten-like hand defences of quilted and sometimes rivet-studded fabric.

▲ Mail and plate helmet

Above: 17th-century, still in use in the service of the cavalry of Tipu Sultan in Mysore in the late 18th century. XXVIA.57

◄ Mail and plate armour (*zereh bagtar*)

Mughal, from Datia, about 1600. XXVIA.148

▲ Pair of arm defences (*dastana*)

From Lahore, early 19th century. They are of steel plates joined by long hinges, and lined with quilted velvet. Inside the embroidered velvet flaps that protect the hands are loops for the fingers and thumb. XXVIA.36

◄ A 19th-century helmet

From Gwalior, decorated with European symbols, probably of the late 18th century. A detail of its mail, constructed of iron, copper and brass links, is shown below. Acquired before 1859. XXVIA.12

FOUR MIRRORS

In the late 18th century this type of armour was replaced by a new type, copied from contemporary Persian armour in which a cuirass of four plates joined by straps, called the *chahar a'ineh*, or 'four mirrors' was worn over a mail shirt (*zereh*). At the same time the manufacture of mail in India changed, from the effective riveted mail which had been used since the early Middle Ages to a far more decorative but ineffective type of mail in which the ends of each link were merely butted together. Different materials (iron, brass and copper) were used for the mail links, grouped together in geometrical or sometimes calligraphic patterns.

◄ Armour of butted mail with a four-plate cuirass (*chahar a'ineh*), helmet and dastana, made in Lahore in the early 19th century. XXVIA.6

FIREARMS

MATCHLOCK MUSKET

◀▼ Matchlock musket (*toradar*)

From Lahore, early 19th century. This gun retains its original slow match, wound around the stock and held in the jaws of the serpentine, as well as its vent pricker, attached to the sling loop by a chain so it did not get lost, and used for cleaning out the vent connecting the priming pan with the breech of the barrel. XXVIF.42

The matchlock musket was probably introduced into India during the Mughal invasions of the 16th century. It continues in use to the present day in remote places such as Chitral, despite the introduction of the flintlock and later percussion firearms by Europeans in the 18th and 19th centuries. The standard Indian form of matchlock musket or *toradar* changed little from the 16th century to the 19th. It was a smooth-bore, muzzle-loading weapon, with a simple sprung and pivoted serpentine directly connected to the trigger, so that when this was pressed the serpentine, with its glowing match-cord, was moved forward into the priming pan to ignite the charge of gunpowder in the breech. The butt of the weapon was characteristically narrow and straight.

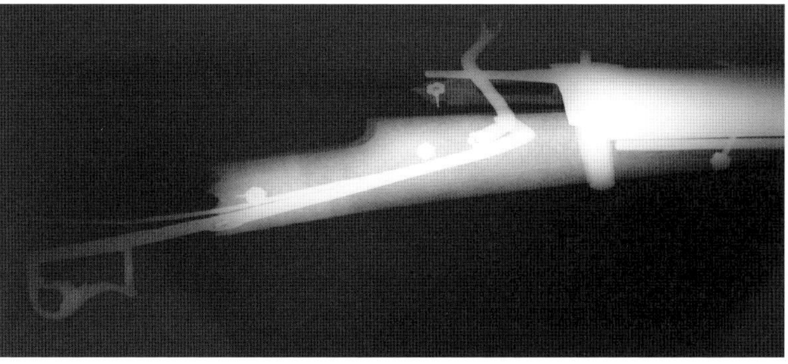

▶ X-ray of the matchlock musket (*toradar*). XXVIF.42

JAZA'IL

A central Asian fashion of stock, with a deep curving and flaring butt, was fashionable in the north west, where they were called *jaza'il.*

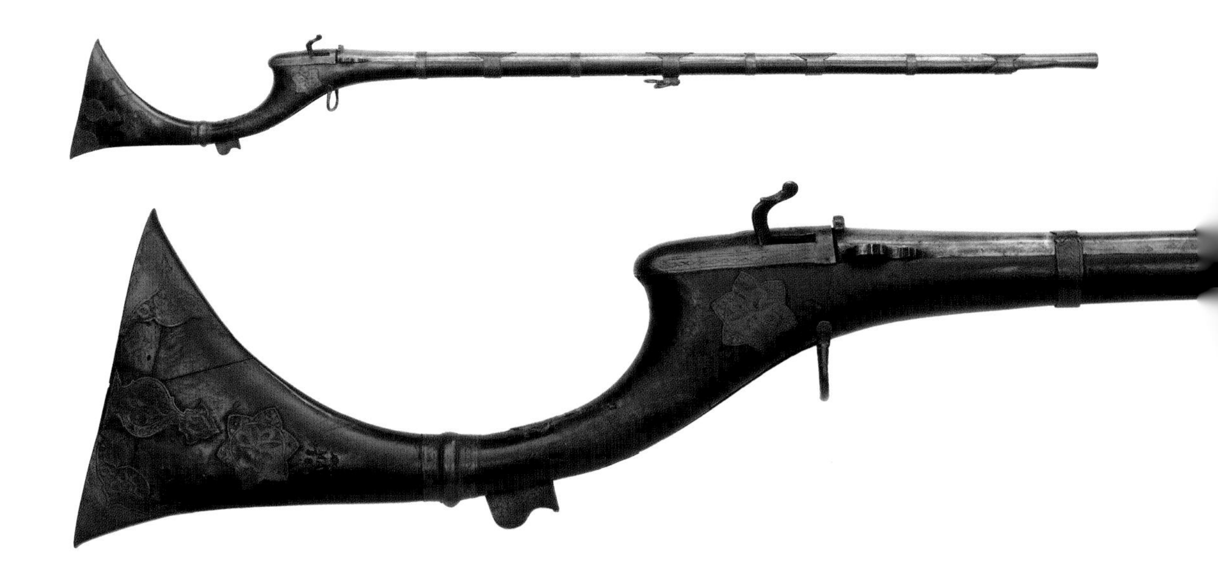

▲ Matchlock musket (*jaza'il*)

Sindh, early 19th century. The stock is decorated with copper plaques and bands. XXVIF.150

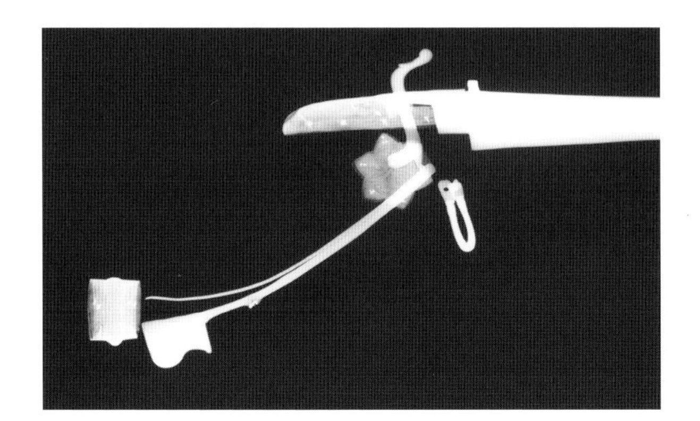

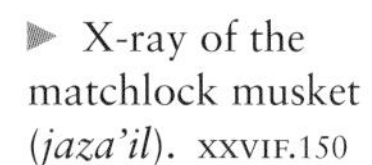

► X-ray of the matchlock musket (*jaza'il*). XXVIF.150

CHANGAL

Larger swivel guns were widely used for defence and attack in sieges, and called *changal.* Some of these were mounted on camels and given the Persian name *zamburak.* (Not illustrated).

REVOLVERS

▼ Matchlock revolving-cylindered gun

Probably 17th century, described by Samuel Colt in his London lecture of 1851. XXVIF.2

Experiments with revolvers, either with a revolving chambered cylinder or a revolving group of barrels, seem to have started quite early in India. They were known to Samuel Colt in his development of the revolver during the early 19th century. The gun shown here was studied by Colt at the Tower of London and illustrated in the text of a lecture on revolver design which he gave in London in 1851.

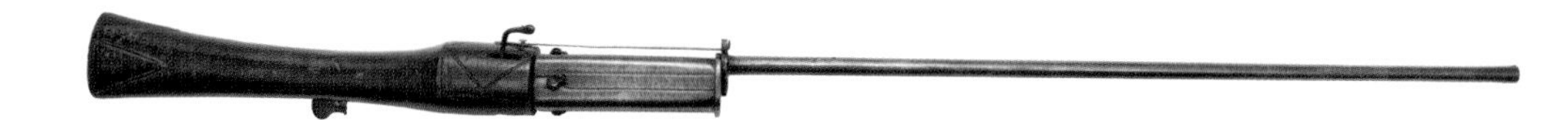

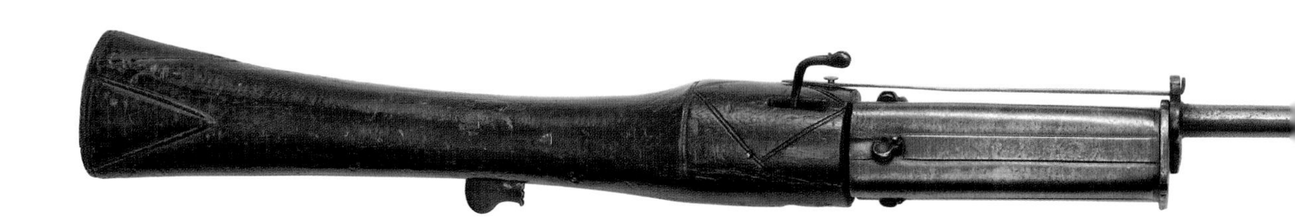

◄ The cylinder, of four chambers, is hand-rotated, and located to the breech by nocks engaging the long narrow top strap which connects the stock to the barrel. XXVIF.2

▲ Belt with silver powder flask and cartouche pouches (*kamr*)

Top: Central Indian, probably from Hyderabad, early 19th century. This style of firearms accoutrements is associated with Arab mercenaries in the employ of the Nizam of Hyderabad in the 19th century. Purchased from the Great Exhibition of 1851. XXVIF.94

▲ Cartridge carrier

Above: From north India, early 19th century. Measured charges of gunpowder were held in the nine tubes of turned ivory with decorative lids. XXVIF.106

FLINTLOCK WEAPONS

Flintlock weapons were introduced by the European powers by the late 17th century. The effectiveness of the musket made for India by the East India Company by the late 18th century led to them being adopted as an emergency measure as the India Pattern musket. These were issued to British infantry throughout the Napoleonic wars. Matchlock pistols are a considerable rarity, and highly impractical, but with the arrival of the flintlock pistols too became common on the sub-continent.

▲ Pair of flintlock pistols

Northern India, possibly Lahore, first half of 19th century. XXVIF.217

◄ Priming flask and cartridge pouches on a matching belt (*kamr*)

Made in Lahore in the early 19th century. XXVIF.136

ARTILLERY

Like hand firearms, gunpowder artillery was introduced into India by the Mughals, and it was used not only for sieges but in pitched battles. At Panipat in 1526 the Mughal artillery was decisive in defeating the army of the Delhi Sultans. Much of the Mughal conquest involved subduing the hill fortresses of Rajasthan, and the use of great cannon, or *tup*, to batter down their defences was key to the success and rapidity of the Mughal conquest. Mughal artillery was influenced by that of the Turks who were pre-eminent in Asia in the field of gunpowder artillery in the 16th and 17th centuries.

▲ Bronze 9-pounder cannon

Cast by G Hutchinson at Cossipore in Calcutta, dated 1838. XIX.247

Mughal miniature of the siege of Ranthambor from the Akbarnama, about 1590. © Victoria and Albert Museum, London

ROCKETS

European developments came to the fore in the 18th century, and the later development of Indian ordnance, especially in the 19th century, was mainly in the hands of British and French artillerists. Rockets had a very long history of military use in India, and the fashion for military rockets in early 19th-century Europe was inspired by Indian models. In the 19th century the Sikhs developed their train of artillery to a very high standard, basing it largely on British ordnance.

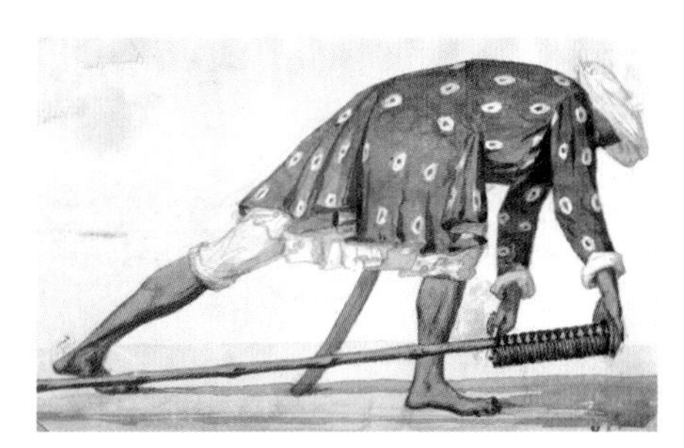

A Mysore rocketeer from the army of Tipu Sultan. From a watercolour by Robert Home. © Victoria and Albert Museum, London

► Bronze gun with carriage and limber

Made in Lahore, about 1840, and used in the First Anglo-Sikh war of 1845–6. XIX.329

▼ Bronze 24-pounder gun

Cast for Tipu Sultan, late 18th century. Found at Kurnool about 1838. XIX.99

ELEPHANT ARMOUR

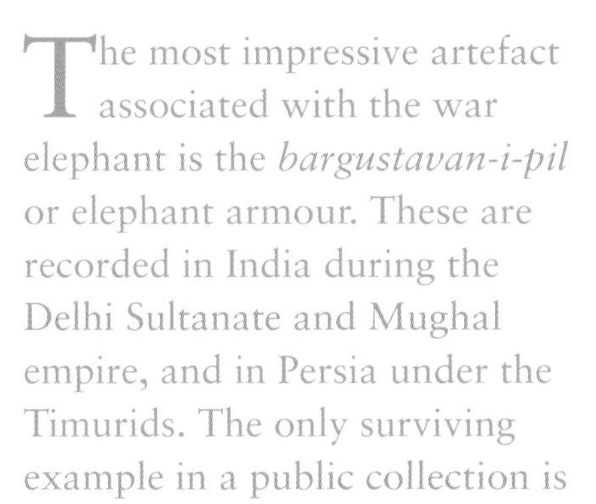

◀ Elephant armour *(bargustavan-i-pil)*

Made of mail and plate, Mughal, probably late 16th or early 17th century. XXVIA.102

▶ Detail showing the construction of mail and plate elephant armour. XXVIA.102

The most impressive artefact associated with the war elephant is the *bargustavan-i-pil* or elephant armour. These are recorded in India during the Delhi Sultanate and Mughal empire, and in Persia under the Timurids. The only surviving example in a public collection is in the Royal Armouries in England. It was probably made in one of the arsenals of the Mughals in north India, in the late 16th or early 17th century, and was acquired in India in 1801 by the second Lord Clive, Earl of Powis. The story that it was taken by the first Lord Clive at the battle of Plassey in 1757, and its consequent 18th-century dating, was pure supposition based on its preservation at Powis Castle.

The armour is of mail and plate construction, and in its present state weighs 142 kg; six of its original eight pieces survive (two of the three panels for the right side are missing) and would originally have weighed 170 kg. The side elements include square panels decorated with embossed trotting elephants, lotus flowers, birds and confronted fish. The armour is otherwise plain except for the scalloped edges of the small plates. Judging by contemporary armours in Mughal miniatures, it was probably covered with fabric except on the square panels and, for the comfort and protection of the elephant for which it was made, was fitted with a padded lining. A pair of cast-iron tusk swords associated with this armour is also in the collection.

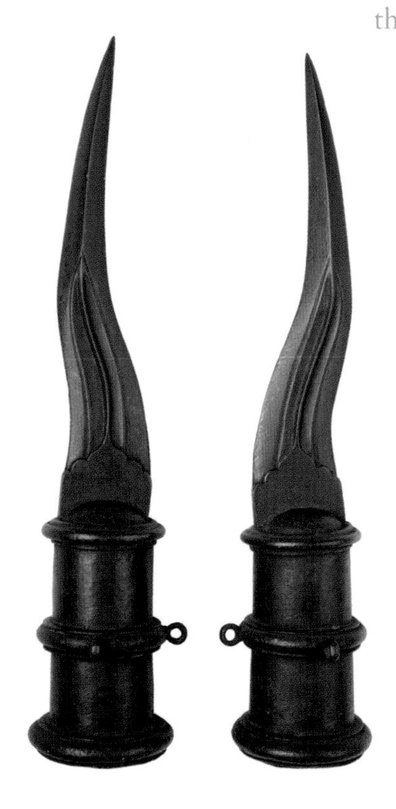

▼ Tusk swords

Associated with the Powis elephant amour. Mughal, probably of late 16th or early 17th century. XXVIM.40

THE PANJAB

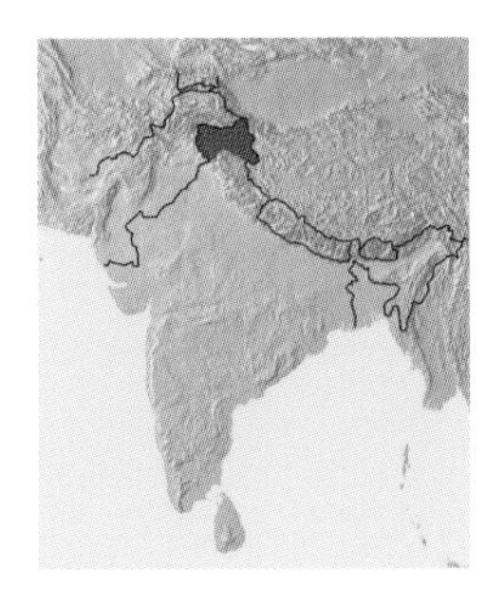

As capital of the Panjab, Lahore was a political and military centre. Under the Mughals it became an important centre for arms manufacture. This continued after the break up of the Mughal empire, and some of the finest arms and armour in the Indian sub-continent were produced in Lahore in the 18th and 19th centuries.

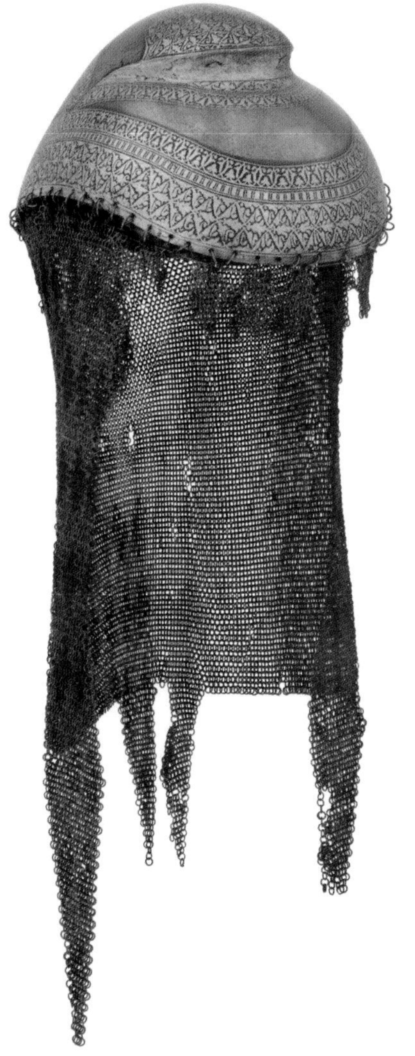

◄ Akali quoit turban (*bunga dastar*)

From Lahore, probably 19th century. XXVIA.60

Sikh religion

The Sikh religion was founded by Guru Nanak (1469–1539). He gained many followers in the Panjab where he was succeeded by a line of Gurus. The word *Sikh* means 'disciple' and *guru* 'spiritual guide'. The distinctive name Singh ('lion') was given to all Sikhs by the tenth Guru, Gobind Singh, in the 18th century. Following his guidance the Sikhs formed an independent state in the Panjab in 1761.

◄ Turban helmet

Made in Lahore, probably early 19th century. The skull is shaped for the Sikh topknot of hair. XXVIA.138

Modernisation of the army

Under its most famous ruler, Ranjit Singh (1792–1839), the Sikh state was expanded to include Kashmir. Its army was modernised with guidance from French advisers. Following two wars with the East India Company (1845–6 and 1848–9), the Panjab was placed under Company administration.

The Sikhs adopted firearms early on, and trained to European military standards they became a respected military force. Some members of the Sikh confederation became enthusiastic religious warriors called *Akalis* (immortals) or *Nihangs*. They wore distinctive blue garments, and high turbans (*bunga dastar*) which carried a number of *chakra*. This was a steel throwing quoit which had been used by some Hindu sects since at least the 16th century, but it became associated particularly with the Akalis. Lahore was an important centre for the arts as well as arms production. The decoration on weapons produced here as well as their general high quality reflects this.

▼ Throwing quoit (*chakra*)

One weapon which was particularly associated with the Sikhs was the steel quoit. With a sharp outer edge, it was spun around on the finger and released to fly off in a given direction accurately. XXVIM.52

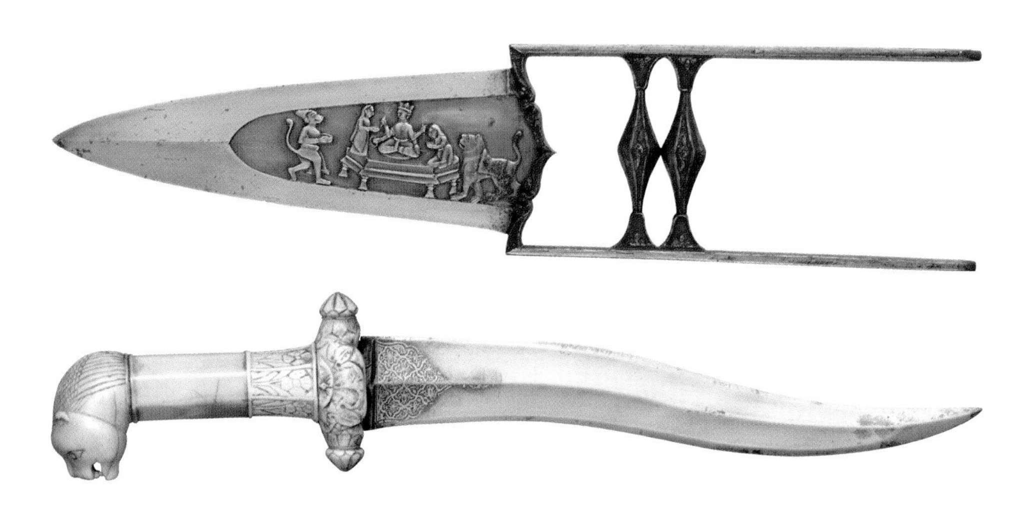

▲ Punch dagger (*katar*)

Above: Early 19th century. The scene of the monkey Hanuman and king Rama is attributed to the Hindu Panjab Hills kingdoms, but the dagger was collected in Indore in the Deccan. XXVID.62

▲ Dagger (*khanjar*)

With an ivory hilt, the pommel carved in the form of a lion's head, probably 18th century. XXVID.74

◄ Axe

From Lahore. Made as an example of the high quality of craftsmanship of the region. Purchased from the Great Exhibition of 1851. XXVIC.41

▲ Shield

Made for Lord Hardinge in Lahore, dated 1847 (1263 AH) in gold koftgari along with Urdu verses on watered steel. XXVIA.79

▼ Matchlock musket (*toradar*)

From Lahore, early 19th century. The wooden stock of this gun is beautifully painted with foliage, and the barrel is decorated in gold koftgari. XXVIF.119

RAJASTHAN

The Rajputs were the principal military class of north India. Despite successive waves of Muslim conquest, Rajasthan remained predominantly Hindu. Rajasthan was never united as an independent state but was divided into a number of small states centred around fortified cities such as Jaipur, Jodhpur, and Udaipur. All of these had their own armouries, several of which survive today.

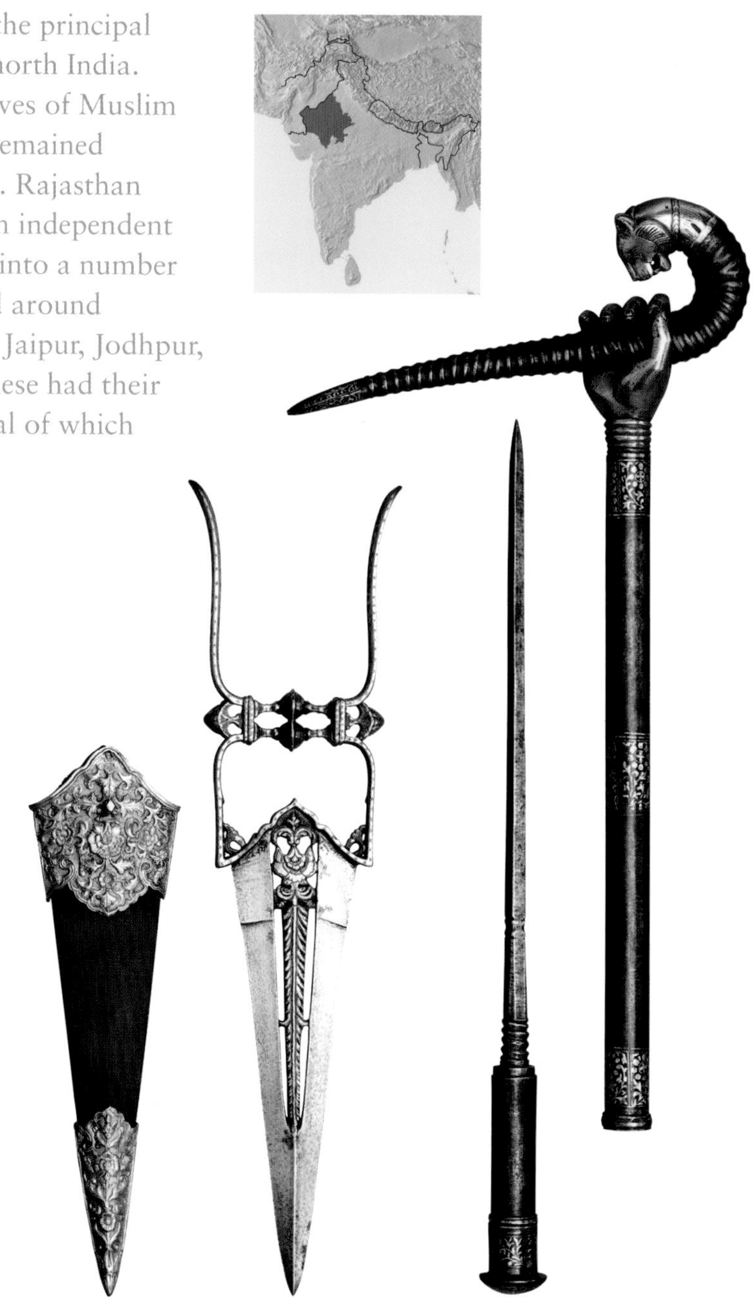

► Punch dagger (*katar*)

From Rajasthan, early 19th century, with a fretted blade. Purchased from the Great Exhibition of 1851. XXVID.83

► 'Fakir's crutch'

Far right: A spiked mace with the spike carved as a blackbuck (*nilgau*) horn with a lion's head at the end, held in a human fist; the stiletto spike is normally concealed, fitting inside the haft of the weapon and unscrewing. Probably from Rajasthan, 18th century. XXVIM.5

► Mace (*gorz*)

Page 57: With a flanged head and an Indian basket-hilt, probably Rajasthan, 18th century. XXVIC.4

KHANDA

The characteristic sword of Rajasthan was the *khanda*. It had a basket hilt with a straight, often leaf-shaped, blade. This sword was so important in Rajput society that it was worshipped in a ritual called the *kharga shapna* during the festival dedicated to the God of War. This example is unusual in being fitted with a pistol alongside the blade and a punch dagger or *katar*. This weapon was made in Rajasthan for the Great Exhibition of 1851 and was acquired following the dispersal of the display.

◀ Straight sword (*khanda*)

With an attached punch dagger (*katar*) and a percussion pistol, Rajasthan, mid 19th century. Purchased from the Great Exhibition of 1851. XXVIS.85

SIND

Situated at the mouth of the river Indus, Sind was the first part of India to come under Muslim rule, in AD 711. It was incorporated into the Mughal empire and changed hands many times until it became independent under Mir Fath 'Ali Khan Talpur. The Talpur family ruled Sind from Hyderabad until 1843, then it was occupied and placed by Sir Charles Napier under East India Company administration.

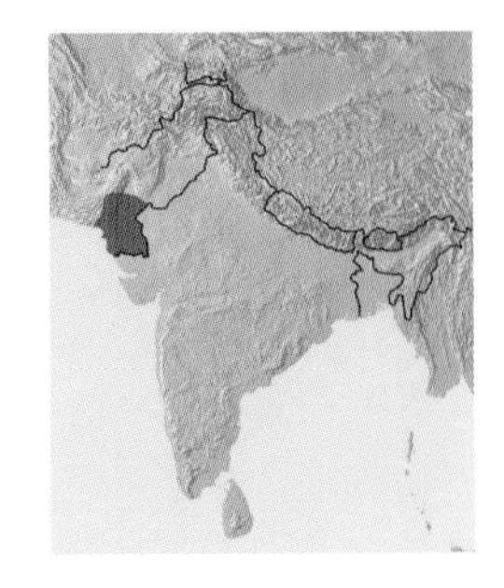

◄ On 17th February 1843 a battle was fought at Miani, Sind, between the Talpur rulers and British forces led by Sir Charles Napier.

Photo by: Universal History Archive/UIG via Getty Images

Sind cavalry

Sind cavalry was unusual in India and the Muslim world in preferring to fight dismounted – sometimes the soldiers were tied together with their sashes to form an unbreakable barrier.

▼ Matchlock rifled musket (*jaza'il*)

From Sind, with the characteristic deeply curved butt of the region.

AL.290.134

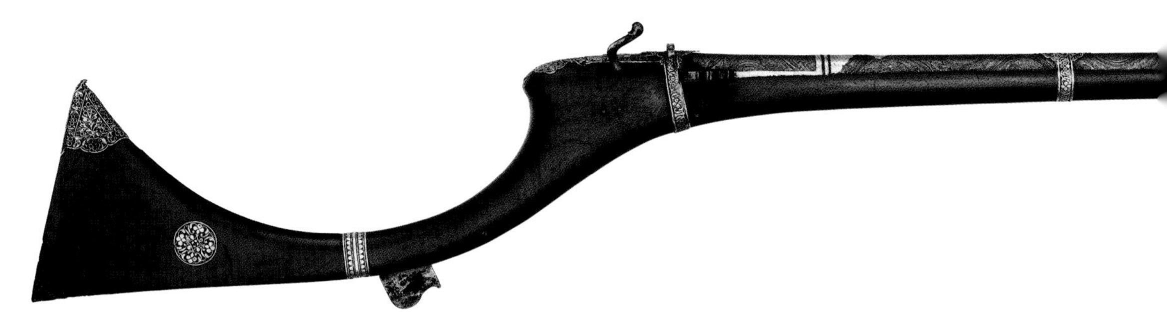

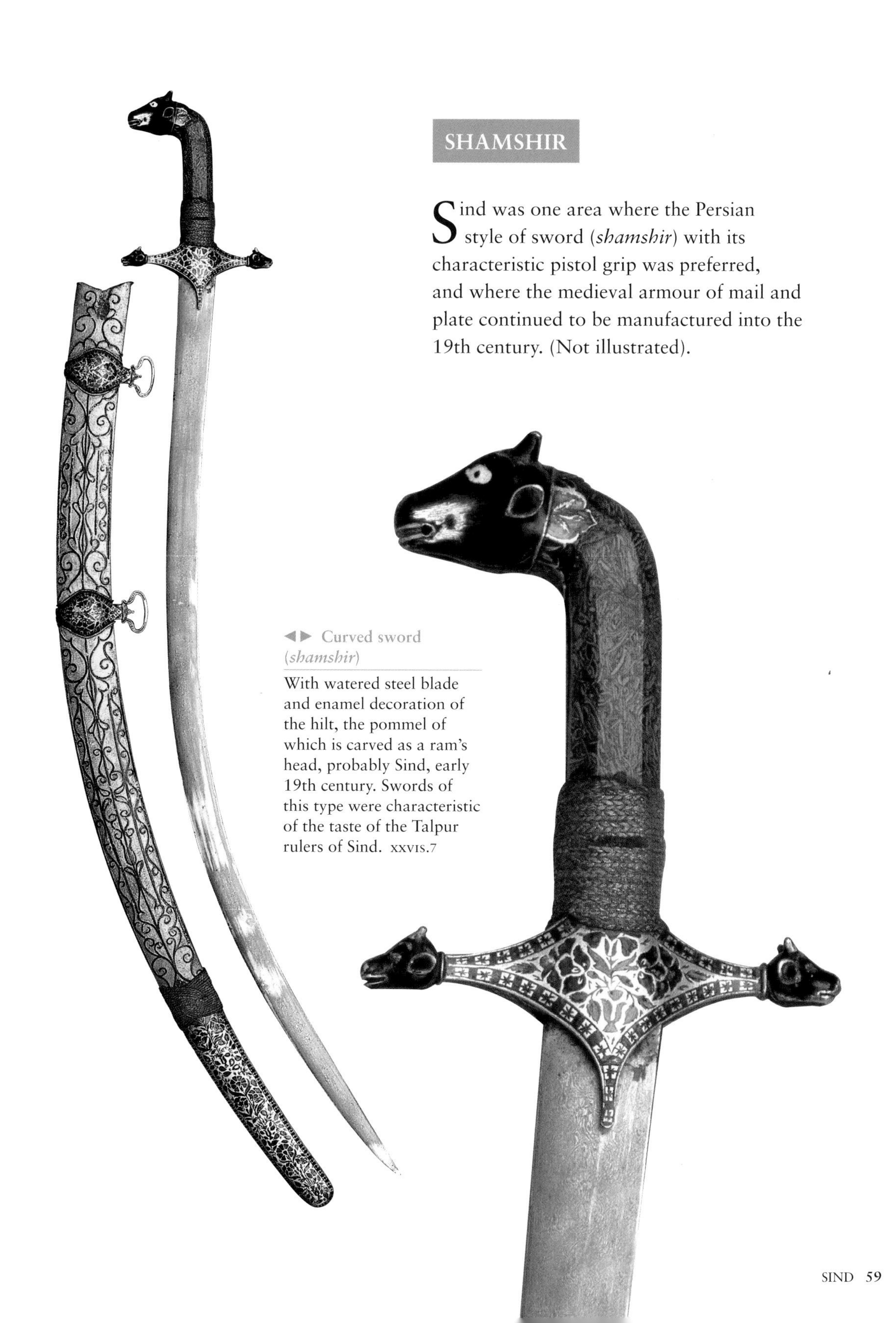

SHAMSHIR

Sind was one area where the Persian style of sword (*shamshir*) with its characteristic pistol grip was preferred, and where the medieval armour of mail and plate continued to be manufactured into the 19th century. (Not illustrated).

◄► Curved sword (*shamshir*)

With watered steel blade and enamel decoration of the hilt, the pommel of which is carved as a ram's head, probably Sind, early 19th century. Swords of this type were characteristic of the taste of the Talpur rulers of Sind. XXVIS.7

GUJARAT

Gujarat, on the west coast of India between the Gulf of Kutch and the Gulf of Cambay, was ruled as an independent Hindu kingdom until it was conquered by the Delhi Sultans under Ala-ud-Din Khiliji in 1297–8. From 1411 it became in independent sultanate until it was conquered by the Mughals of Akbar in 1576. It had always been important in sea-borne trade with the West, and Europeans established trading stations along its coast. The British East India Company founded a station at Surat in 1614, and the company took over political control from the Mahrattas in the Second Anglo-Mahratta War of 1803–5.

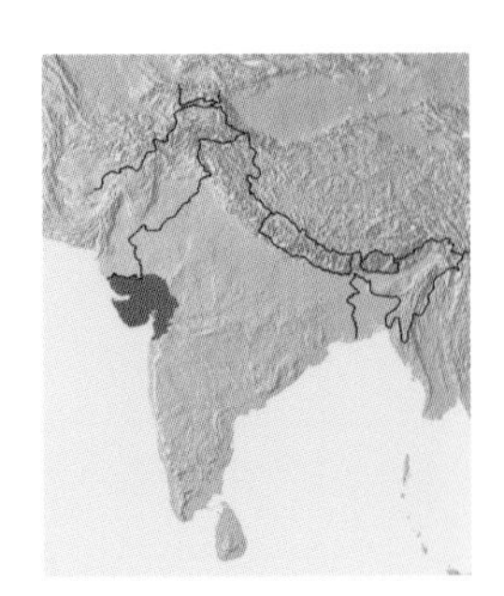

CUMBERJUNG

The *cumberjung* is a unique weapon in the Royal Armouries collection, a double-ended flail with sharpened quoits attached to the chains.

▼ *Cumberjung*

Gujarat, early 19th century. The haft is gripped at either end and the quoits whirled around on their chains at either side of the user. XXVIC.49

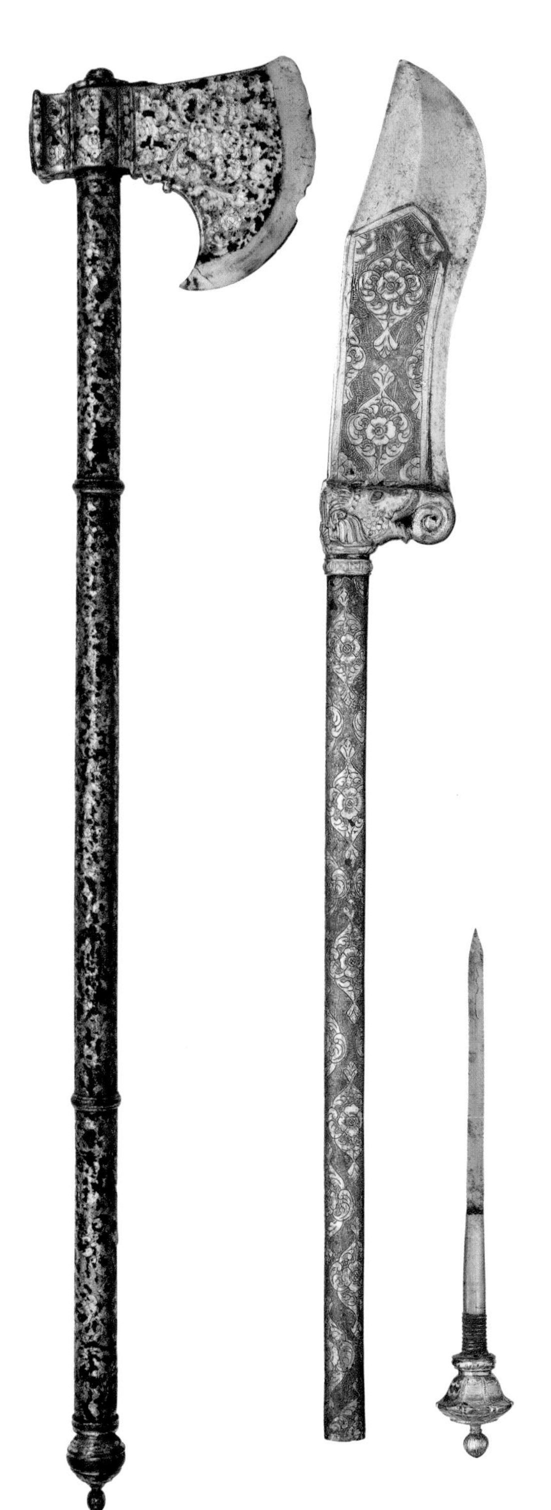

BHUJ

The characteristic weapon of Gujarat is an axe with a heavy dagger-like blade springing from an elephant head. These weapons are often called *bhuj* after the town in Kutch with which they are associated.

◄ Axe (*bhuj or buckie*)

Gujarat, early 19th century.
Acquired before 1859. XXVIC.38

◄ Saddle axe (*tabarzin*)

Left: Gujarat, early 19th century.
Acquired before 1859. XXVIC.39

THE DECCAN

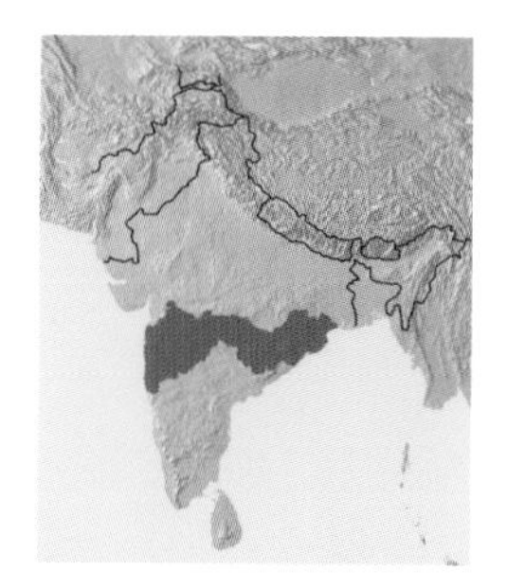

The Deccan is the vast plateau of rugged country covering most of central and southern India. Much of this area was absorbed as part of the Mughal Empire, but when Mughal influence declined after the rule of Aurangzeb, strong successor states were established in the Deccan. The arms and armour produced in this area were fairly distinctive, combining influences from the Mughal culture predominant in the north of India with the heavy metalwork decoration that was a dominant tendency amongst the weaponry of the south.

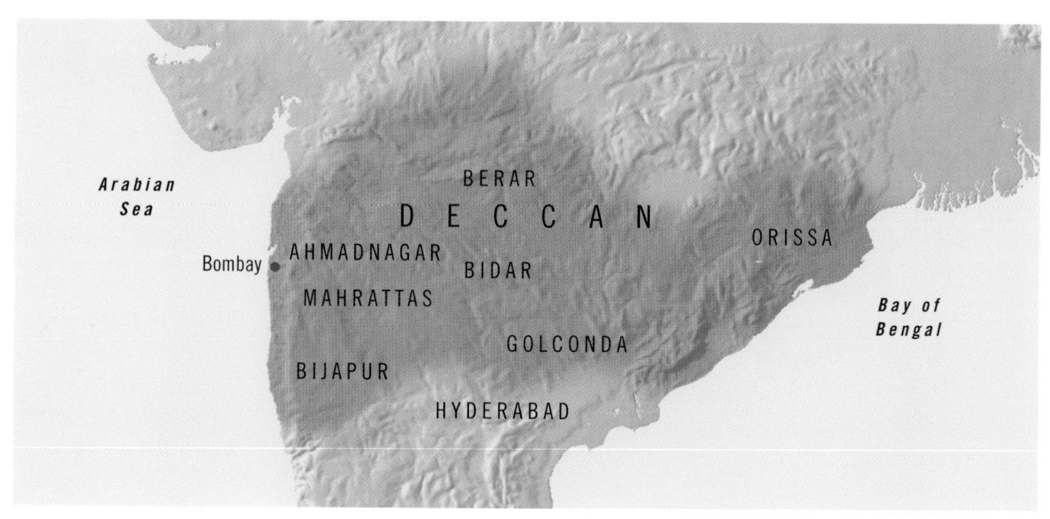

▲ The Deccan.

The Deccan Sultanates

In order to subjugate the Deccan, the Mughals had to conquer numerous independent sultanates between the fourteenth and seventeenth centuries. Bijapur sultanate capitulated in 1689 after the Mughal general Anup Singh captured the fort at Adoni. Afterwards, large quantities of arms and armour were transported to the Mughal arsenal at Bikanir in Rajasthan where they were stored until the twentieth century, thus providing an invaluable insight into the style of the military equipment of the Deccan.

◀ Shaffron

Detail of fretted metalwork. XXVIH.36

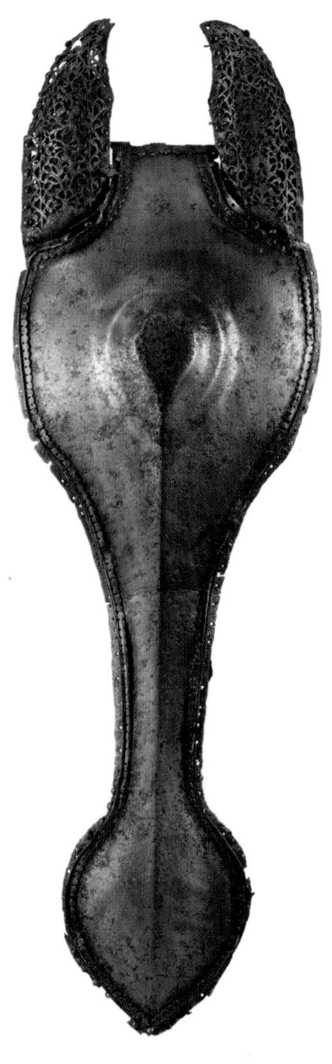

▲ Shaffron

Early 17th century, with fretted metalwork on the ear defences showing peacocks in vegetation. XXVIH.36

► Mail and plate coat (*zereh bagtar*)

17th century, with long skirts and heavy mail on the upper chest. The Devanagari inscription on the front plate describes how this shirt was obtained after Maharajah Anup Singh besieged the fort of Adoni in 1689. There is also the name 'Darvish Sahib' in Urdu. XXVIA.291

▲ Turban helmet

Probably late 16th century, modified with nasal, neckguard, peak and missing cheekpieces in the 17th century. This helmet came from the Bikanir arsenal, but the shape of the bowl and the *makhara* finial of the nasal makes it different from helmets thought to originate from Bikanir; it is probably a Deccan product. XXVIA.332

► Sword (*firanghi*)

17th century, formed entirely from steel with a European rapier blade. Acquired from the Bikanir arsenal but probably captured in the Deccan. XXVIS.402

The Mahrattas

Under the leadership of Sivaji, the Mahrattas formed their own state and began to defy Mughal authority even before the death of Aurangzeb. By the end of the 18th century, the Mahrattas held sway over most of central India. The Mahratta cavalry tended to be less heavily armoured than the Mughal armies, which allowed them greater mobility in the hilly terrain of the Deccan. The preferred arms for cavalry and infantry were a sword and shield and either a spear or a matchlock; the bow was also still carried by many. The *pata*, or gauntlet sword, is often considered to be a predominantly Mahratta weapon, suited for use on horseback due to its length. A high level of expertise was required to wield the *pata* effectively because the wrist was locked in place by the gauntlet, but contemporary accounts describe how Mahratta warriors demonstrated great skill whilst fencing with them.

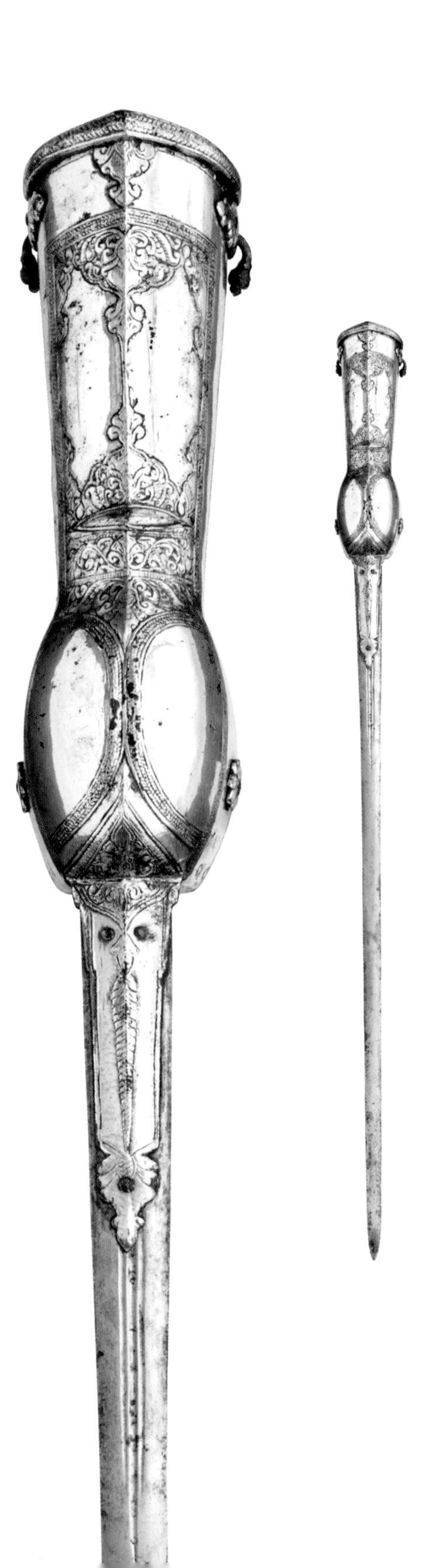

► Sword (*pata*)

18th century, with an iron gauntlet decorated with panels and foliage, and a European blade. XXVIS.240

► Spear

Page 67: 18th century. The spearhead and mounts on the black wood shaft are elaborately decorated with silver gilt flowers and foliage; the shaft unscrews, presumably for practicality when not in use. XXVIL.222

◄ Sword (*firanghi*)

18th century, with a European blade and an Indian basket hilt. This sword was originally shown in the Great Exhibition in 1851, where it was acquired for the Armouries with other material from the Indian Courts. XXVIS.79

Hyderabad State

Although the Nizam of Hyderabad was originally a vassal of the Mughal Empire, Hyderabad State broke free from Mughal supremacy soon after the death of Aurangzeb and became established as an independent kingdom. Once Britain assumed political control of India, the Nizams remained as client kings and retained control of internal governance of Hyderabad State until 1947.

▼ Sword (*talwar*)

Mid-18th century, possibly made for Muzaffar Jang of Hyderabad (r.1750–1). XXVIS.205

▲ Dagger (*bichwa*)

18th century, with a heavily reinforced point, decorated with silver koftgari. XXVID.48

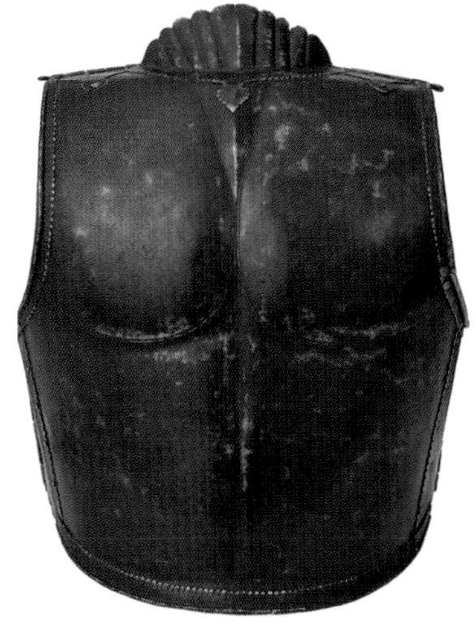

▲ Cuirass

Dated 1192 AH (1778–9 AD). The full breastplate and backplate gives this cuirass a form more usually associated with Europe. The inscription shows that it is from the arsenal of Nizam 'Ali Khan (the second Nizam, r.1762 – 1803). There are numerous examples of these cuirasses, all vey similar in appearance, suggesting that they were manufactured for a body of troops. XXVIA.338

► Cuirass

Late 18th century. Another more highly decorated example of an armour with full breastplate and backplate; this style was popular in Hyderabad until the 19th century. XXVIA.112

MYSORE: THE ARMS AND ARMOUR OF TIPU SULTAN

The Sultanate of Mysore was an important Muslim successor kingdom in the south of India. The kingdom was founded by a military adventurer, Haidar 'Ali Khan, in 1756. During the process of its expansion he came into conflict with the Mahrattas and with the British East India Company. In 1780 he and his son, Tipu Sultan, inflicted a crushing defeat on the British at the battle of Polliliur (Kanchipuram). During the struggle for empire between the French and the British in the south of India, the Sultans of Mysore allied with the French. Tipu Sultan was defeated by the forces of the East India Company at the siege of his capital, Seringapatam (or Srirangapatna) in 1799.

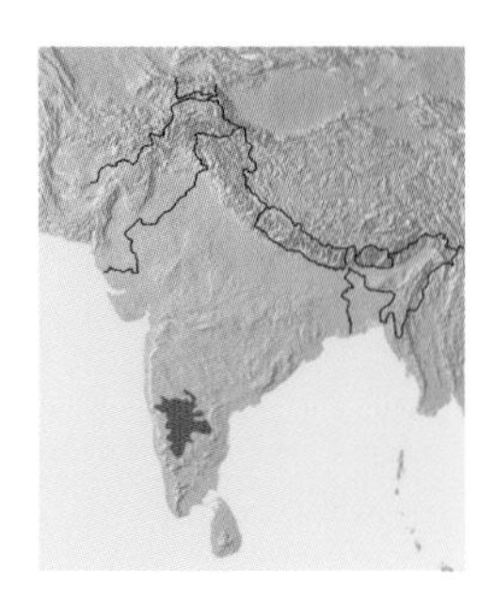

► Armour (*peti*) of Tipu Sultan

Page 71: Made of quilted fabric covered in embroidered velvet.
XXVIA.139

TIPU'S ARSENAL

Tipu's arsenal included weapons of the highest quality, often imitating European types. His army was drilled by French military advisers, who were also responsible for some of the European influences on their equipment. The army itself was heterogeneous, and included Afghans and Arabs as well as local troops. The arms and armour from Tipu's personal armoury reveal an interesting mixture of ancient and modern styles. His personal armour, an example of which is preserved in the Royal Armouries, is of fabric and the descendant of a very ancient form of Indian armour. His firearms, though made by Indian gunsmiths in his factory at Seringapatam, were copies of the most modern European guns and had all the latest features.

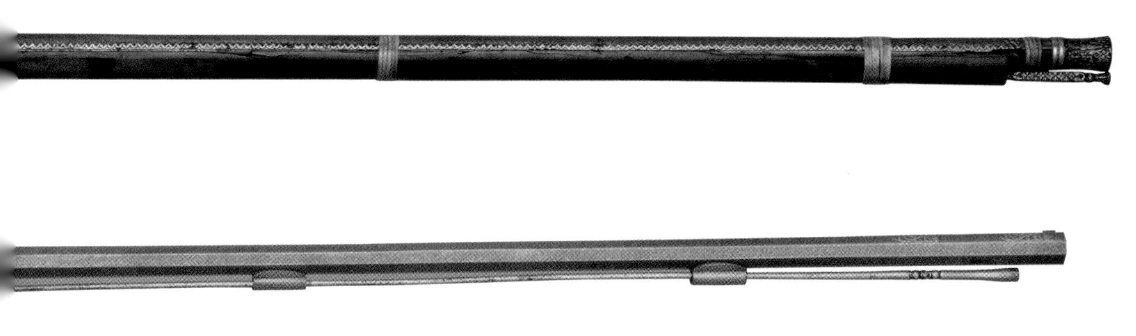

▼ Sword (*talwar*)

The blade is inlaid with an Imperial umbrella, from Mysore, late 18th century, purchased from the Codrington collection, 1863. XXVIS.99

▲ Flintlock sporting gun

Made in England and decorated in Mysore, dated 1784 (1212 AM). XXVIF.102

▲ Matchlock musket (*toradar*)

Top: With a tiger picked out in *koftgari* on the trigger. From Mysore, 18th century. XXVIF.101

Tiger of Mysore

Tipu is known as the 'Tiger of Mysore', because of his use of the tiger stripe (*bubri*) motif as a form of decoration that was applied to everything in the Sultanate.
His personal swords had hilts in the form of tigers' heads, his soldiers were uniformed in 'tiger jackets', decorated with tiger stripes, and even their bayonets had blades in the form of tiger stripes. A bronze mortar in the Royal Armouries collection is cast in the form of a seated tiger, and his other artillery pieces are decorated with the ubiquitous *bubri*.

► Bayonet (*sangin*)

Made in Mysore in the form of tiger stripes (*bubri*) with tiger head sockets, late 18th century. XXVID.27

► Bronze mortar (*deg*)

Cast in the form of a tiger for Tipu Sultan. Found at Kurnool on the north eastern border of the Mysore kingdom about 1838. XIX.119

SOUTH INDIA

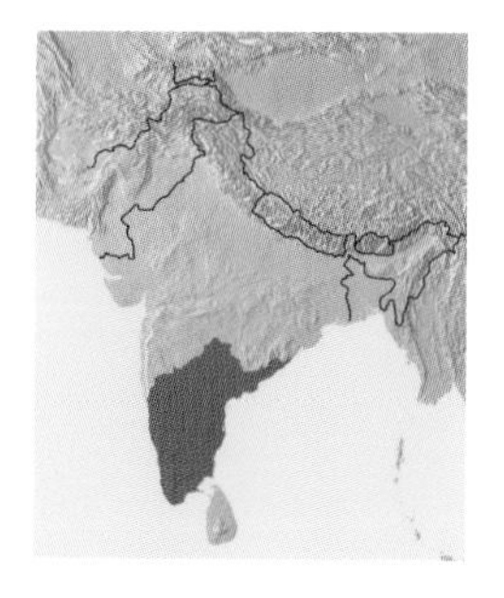

During the late 18th century, the latest military technology was deployed in the Sultanate of Mysore, but in the rest of south India the arms and armour were very conservative. The medieval Indian straight and flamboyant swords continued to be used until the 20th century and a number of peculiar weapon forms survived.

SWORDS

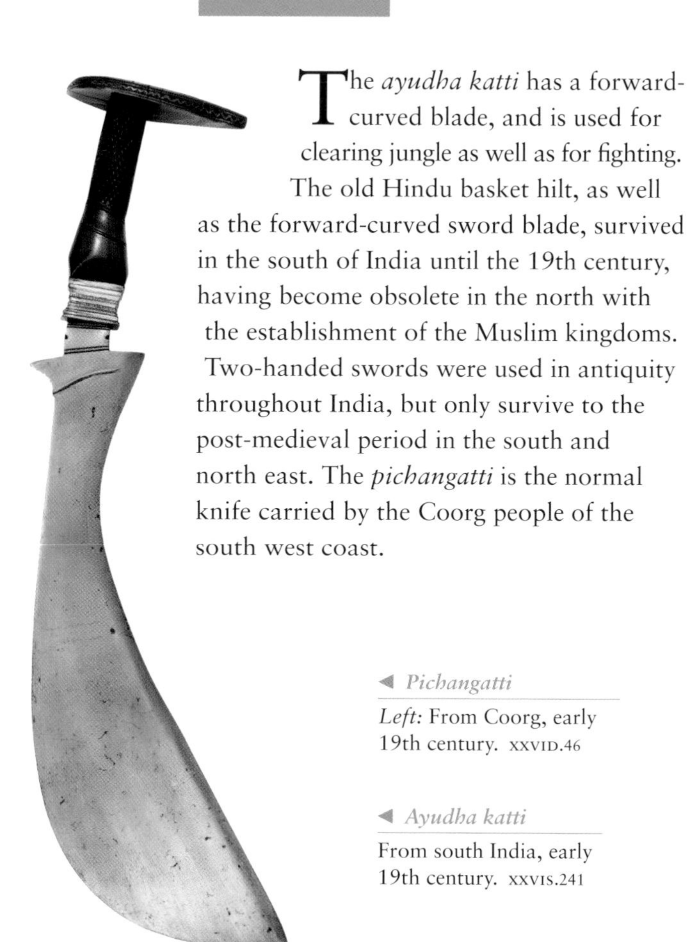

The *ayudha katti* has a forward-curved blade, and is used for clearing jungle as well as for fighting. The old Hindu basket hilt, as well as the forward-curved sword blade, survived in the south of India until the 19th century, having become obsolete in the north with the establishment of the Muslim kingdoms. Two-handed swords were used in antiquity throughout India, but only survive to the post-medieval period in the south and north east. The *pichangatti* is the normal knife carried by the Coorg people of the south west coast.

◄ *Pichangatti*

Left: From Coorg, early 19th century. XXVID.46

◄ *Ayudha katti*

From south India, early 19th century. XXVIS.241

► Sword

South Indian flamboyant sword, possibly 17th century. XXVIS.207

▼ *Vercheroval*

From Coorg, probably 18th century. It is decorated with a narrow band of applied brass along the back, together with a band of scrolling foliage and flowers, and a large rosette, near the hilt. XXVIS.243

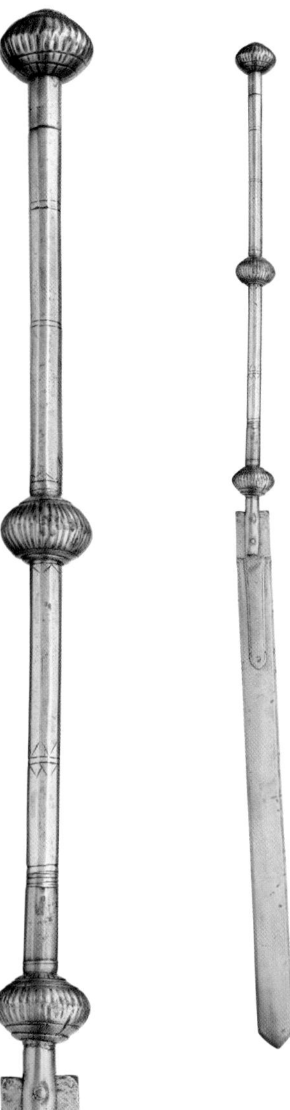

▲ Two handed sword

Early 19th century. Southern India. Made entirely of polished steel. The grip takes the form of a long facetted bar on which are three fluted knops, one forming the pommel, another above the blade and the third between the two hands. XXVIS.130

PARRYING WEAPONS

Parrying weapons (*madu*) are made of pairs of horns, usually blackbuck (*nilgau*), with sharpened or reinforced points fastened together by pairs of rivets and often fitted with a small round shield.

► *Madu*

Made of blackbuck horns, probably Mysore, dated 1758/9. Purchased from the Codrington collection, 1863. XXVIM.10

MUSKETS

South Indian muskets used forward-acting snap-matchlock mechanisms, probably introduced by the Spanish in the 16th century.

► Matchlock musket (*toradar*)

Of typical Coorg form, early 19th century. Presented by the Secretary of State for India to the Rotunda Museum of Artillery, Woolwich, 1869. XXVIF.153

THROWING STICK

The throwing stick (*katariya*) was also known as a '*birra jungee*', and is similar to the boomerang. It was used principally for hunting hares and birds.

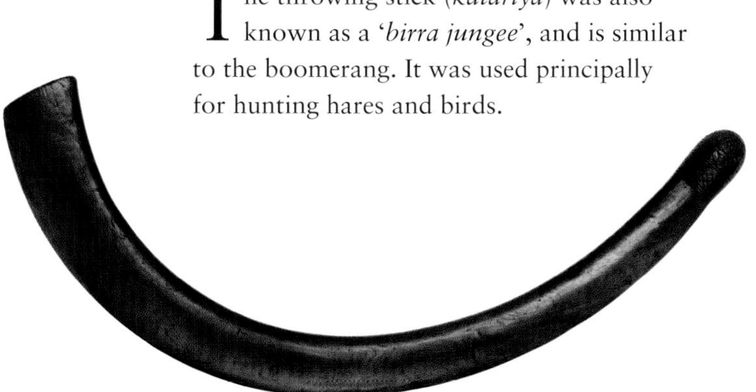

► Throwing stick (*katariya*)

From Hyderabad, early 19th century. Purchased from the Codrington collection, 1863. XXVIM.20

SRI LANKA

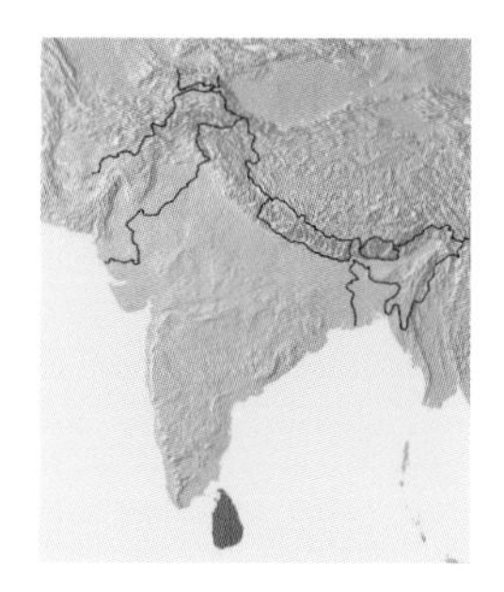

Sri Lanka was never of great military importance internationally, but it did develop distinctive weapons. These include the dagger, *piha kaetta*, and the sword, *kastane*. It is curious that the blades of these weapons were often imported from Europe even though in the Middle Ages Sri Lanka had its own important steel industry. Sri Lanka produced watered crucible steel (*wootz*) of the highest quality, and probably exported much of its output to Islamic western Asia.

KASTANE

The characteristic sword of Sri Lanka is the *kastane*, with its short, curved (and often imported) blade, and dragon-headed hilt. Some surviving examples can be dated to the 17th century, where they had a brief vogue as fashionable swords in England and the Netherlands; the Parliamentarian Colonel Alexander Popham was evidently proud to wear one in his great equestrian portrait formerly preserved at Littlecote House (*see page 78*).

◀▶ Sword (*kastane*)

The characteristic sword of Sri Lanka, early 19th century. Acquired before 1859. XXVIS.167

▲ Portrait of the mid 17th century of Colonel Alexander Popham in cuirassier's armour, wearing a Sri Lankan *kastane*, from the Littlecote House collection. I.315

► Sword (*kastane*)

Sri Lankan, 1758, with a European blade. XXVIS.395

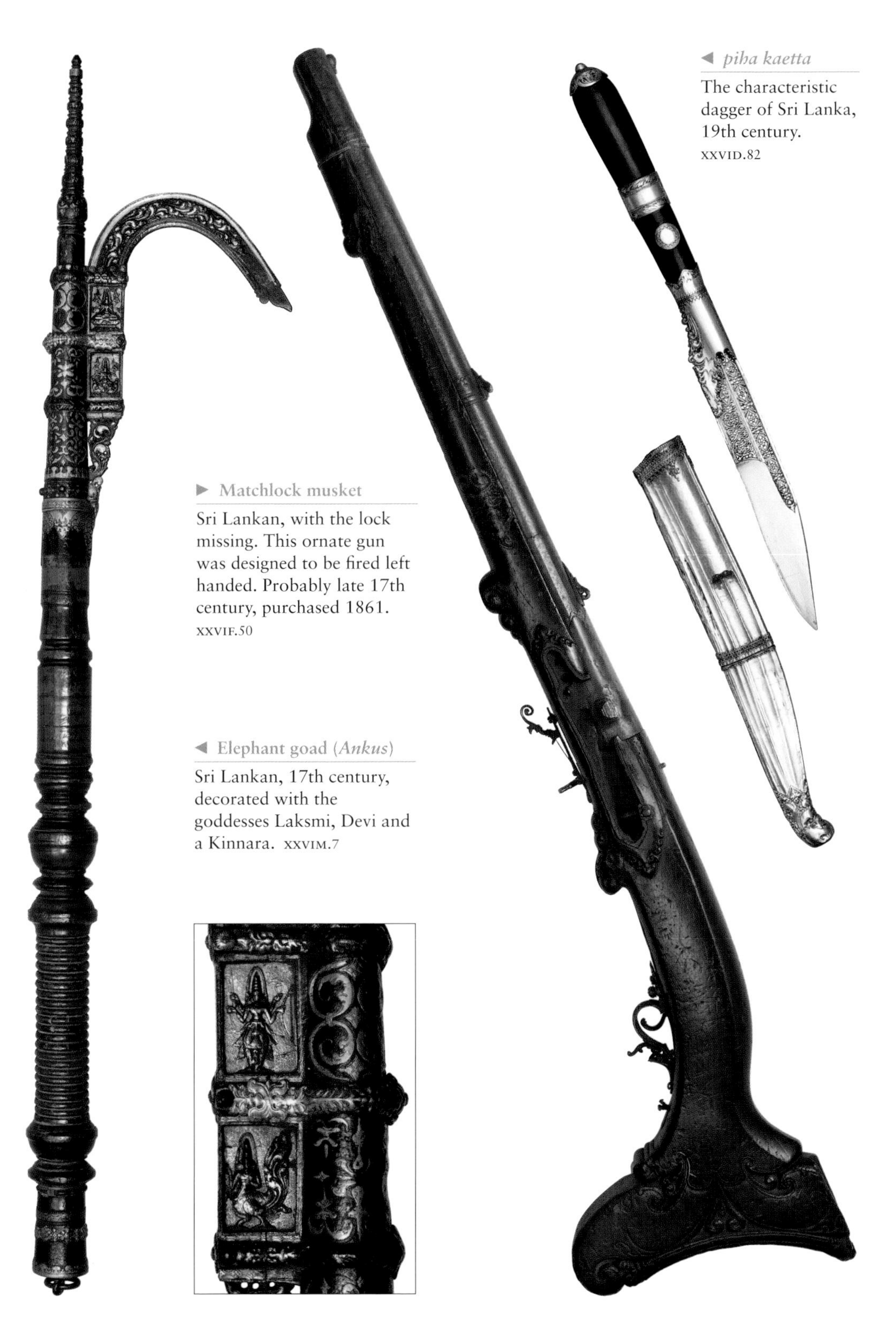

◄ *piha kaetta*

The characteristic dagger of Sri Lanka, 19th century. XXVID.82

► Matchlock musket

Sri Lankan, with the lock missing. This ornate gun was designed to be fired left handed. Probably late 17th century, purchased 1861. XXVIF.50

◄ Elephant goad (*Ankus*)

Sri Lankan, 17th century, decorated with the goddesses Laksmi, Devi and a Kinnara. XXVIM.7

EUROPEANS IN INDIA

While European involvement in India before 1700 was restricted to trade, the 18th century saw a major change. The trading establishments of the European states, in particular Britain and France, grew to the extent of being able to support private armies and carry on full-scale warfare with the Indian states and with each other, and the military developments in Europe were naturally brought to the field of battle in India. This in turn led the Indian states to hire European military consultants in order to modernise and gain an edge on their neighbours.

Claude Martin

An example of this process is seen in the life of Claude Martin. Martin enlisted into the French army only to be captured by the East India Company army at Pondicherry near Madras in 1761. Joining the Company army he rose by 1796 to the rank of general. He also became a close friend of the Nawab of Awadh, and in 1776 was appointed super-intendent of the Nawab's arsenal at Lucknow, incidentally becoming one of the richest Europeans in India. Martin developed Lucknow arsenal into a manufactory of weapons and ordnance for the Nawab's army, and also catered for his master's taste for technical, scientific and artistic objects, making a number of repeating flintlock guns, one of which he presented to the king of France.

◀▶ Processional sword of the state of Awadh

Early 19th century. The decoration of the blade with European armorials combined with the fish badge of Awadh illustrates the influence of men like Martin on the Indian states. XXVIS.153

▲ Pair of miniature bronze 2.25 in howitzers

By Claude Martin, made at Lucknow about 1786. XIX.292–3

◄ Portrait of Claude Martin

From La Martiniere College prize medal, bronze, about 1865, Lucknow. XVIII.331

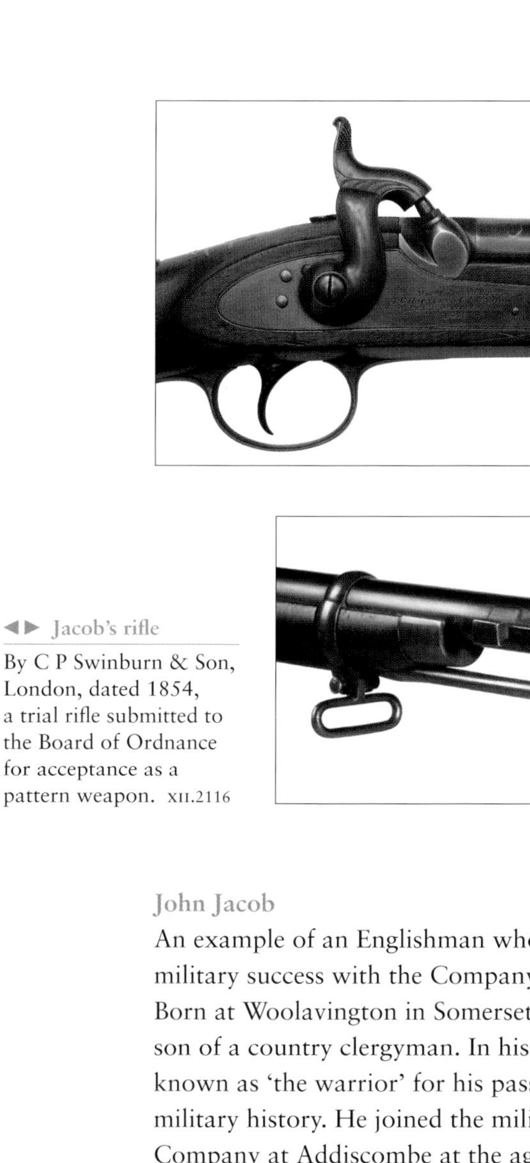

◄► Jacob's rifle

By C P Swinburn & Son, London, dated 1854, a trial rifle submitted to the Board of Ordnance for acceptance as a pattern weapon. XII.2116

John Jacob

An example of an Englishman who saw considerable military success with the Company in India is John Jacob. Born at Woolavington in Somerset in 1812, Jacob was the son of a country clergyman. In his childhood he was known as 'the warrior' for his passionate interest in military history. He joined the military seminary of the Company at Addiscombe at the age of 14, in 1828 joined the Bombay Artillery, and soon acquired a reputation as a fine engineer and a fearless cavalry commander. Jacob eventually commanded two regiments of native infantry, 'Jacob's rifles', and three of cavalry, the Scinde Irregular Horse, later simply Jacob's Horse. In weapons studies he is best known for his efforts to develop a successful military rifle. He believed the ideal military rifle should be double-barrelled with four-groove rifling and fire a winged projectile, and he had a number of prototypes made and submitted to the Board of Ordnance for acceptance into general service with the British army.

▲ *Tent Club at Tiffin*, illustration by Percy Carpenter from *Hog Hunting in Lower Bengal*. London, 1861.

British colony

During Queen Victoria's reign British attitudes towards India became more colonial. Before then British administrators had identified with the country, adopting Indian ways, often taking Indian wives. But by the 1830s this attitude was changing. Increasing numbers of colonial officers now tended to marry their own nationality, thereby becoming more remote from the native Indians. Thus the British largely rejected assimilation in favour of the privileged lifestyle of the conqueror.

◄ Cavalry trooper's sword

Late 18th century. Probably supplied to the East India Company. It bears the 'crowned W' inspection mark associated with Lt. Col. Windus. IX.253

◄▲ *Above: Sepoys at rifle practice.*

Page 84: Hodson's Horse at Rhotuck.

Both images from *The Campaign in India 1857-1858 from drawings made during the eventful period of the Great Mutiny, illustrating the military operations before Delhi and its neighbourhood,* colour lithographs by George Francklin Atkinson and others. Published by Day and Son, London, 1859.

The Indian Mutiny

The Indian Mutiny (as the British called it), the Sepoy Rebellion or Sepoy War, of 1857–9, was a culmination of events that played on the religious fears of Hindus and Muslims in Bengal, Awadh, and Panjab. At the time of the rebellion, British authority in India was exercised by the East India Company through an army of 34,000 European troops – divided into soldiers of the regular British Army and those of the Company. All Company weapons bore a distinctive Lion mark. There were also 257,000 native soldiers, or Sepoys, in three armies: Madras, Bombay, and, the largest, the Bengal Army. It was in this last that the mutiny broke out.

Causes of the mutiny

In 1857 it was decided to replace the smooth-bore percussion musket, used by most regiments in India, with the muzzle-loading Enfield percussion rifle. The new weapon used a greased paper cartridge

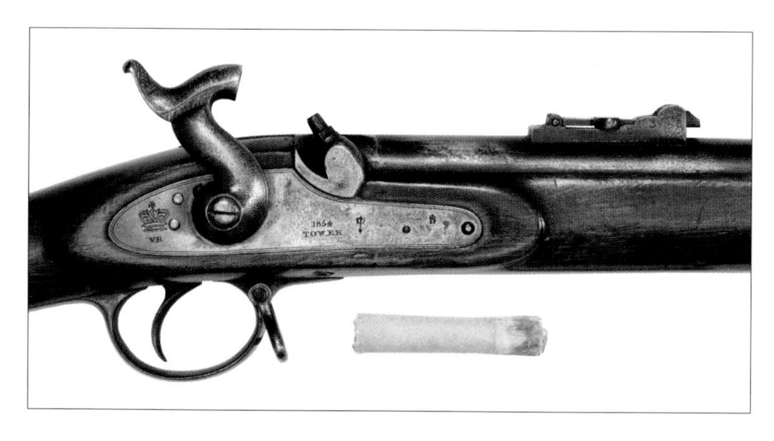

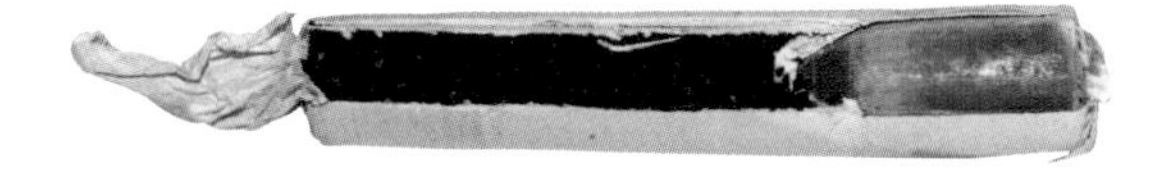

▲► Pattern 1853 rifled musket

Dated 1854. Issue to the Sepoys of this new pattern of musket sparked the 'Indian Mutiny' of 1857. XII.9002

▲ Cartridge

For the Pattern 1853 rifled musket. XX.2207

to hold its main charge of black powder and a special lead bullet. When the rifle was loaded the end of the cartridge had to be bitten off, the powder poured down the barrel, and the bullet rammed down after it. A rumour started that the grease was a mixture of beef and pork fat, the use of which was against the religious beliefs of the Hindu and Muslim Sepoys respectively. This added to existing fears that the British wanted to force them to become Christian.

End of the East India Company

Discontent became rebellion in May 1857 when the Sepoys at Meerut mutinied. They killed many of their British officers and then marched on Delhi. After taking the city, they proclaimed Bahadur Shah II, the last of the Mughal emperors, their leader. More mutinies followed: in Lucknow, Rhohilkand, the Ganges valley, Rajputana, central India, and Cawnpore (Kanpur). The British, with the help of Sikhs and Gurkhas, responded with campaigns in Delhi, the province of Oudh (Awadh), and in central India.

▲ *The Baillie Guard Battery and Hospital* from *Sketches and Incidents of the siege of Lucknow* by CH Mecham, 1858.

Delhi, the ancient capital of India, was vital to the British cause. It was recaptured after a long siege. In Oudh the British attempted to relieve the besieged garrisons at Lucknow and Cawnpore. Lucknow held out till it was relieved; the Cawnpore garrison surrendered but was massacred. In central India the campaign focused on the capture of Jhansi. Here too British authority was eventually re-imposed and the mutineers defeated. In 1859, after the rebellion, the East India Company was wound up and henceforth India was ruled from London by the British Government. In 1876 Queen Victoria was proclaimed Empress of India.

The British leave India

The Indian army, re-organized after the Mutiny, played a key part in the maintenance of the British Empire and the projection of Britain's power abroad. The army fought in China during the Boxer rebellion, and in France and the Middle East during the First World War. In the Second World War Indians served in Africa, Italy and the Far East. By the end of the Second World War the clamour and pressure for Indian independence was over-whelming. In 1947, after 347 years in India, the British left, leaving behind two countries, India and Pakistan.

Persia under the Safavids

THE ROYAL ARMOURIES' COLLECTION

◀ View of the Oriental Gallery at Leeds.

Armour of the Great Mogul?

When the first public displays were constructed at the Tower of London in 1660, at the time of the restoration of the monarchy under King Charles II, the 'armour of the Great Mogul' formed part of the collection that crowd flocked to see. Unfortunately geography had become slightly muddled, and the armour in question was in fact one of the Japanese armours presented as diplomatic gifts to King James I in 1613 by Tokugawa Hidetada, son of Tokugawa Ieyasu the Shogun of Japan.

The Norman Crusader

▲ The 'Norman Crusader', composed of Mughal Indian mail and plate armours for man and horse. From Charles Knight (ed.), *Old England: A Pictorial Museum of Royal, Ecclesiastical, Municipal, Baronial and Popular Antiquities, Vol. I.* London; James Sangster and Co, 1864.

Bullock Museum

The Indian collection at the Tower actually began in 1833 with the purchase of the 'Norman crusader'. This was the armoured figure, purportedly of a European crusading knight, which had graced Bullock's Museum in Liverpool in the early 19th century, and had previously been in the cabinet assembled by the Reverend Green of Lichfield. In 1809 the success of the Bullock Museum in Liverpool led it to be moved to London where it opened in Regent Street. During the move, 'The Norman Crusader' had acquired an armoured horse, which some said had been made for Bullock from an elephant armour. The museum fell on hard times, changed hands and the collection was ultimately auctioned off, and the Tower acquired the 'Crusader', having identified it as a rare and interesting example of early Indian armour (see page 16).

East India Company gift

The real foundation of the Indian collection came in 1851–1853 with a gift from the East India Company. The impetus behind this acquisition seems to have come primarily from the interest of the British public in the hard-fought Anglo-Sikh wars of the 1840s, which prompted a great deal of respect for the Sikhs as worthy opponents. The Master of Ordnance personally requested that representative samples of Indian arms and armour be gathered by

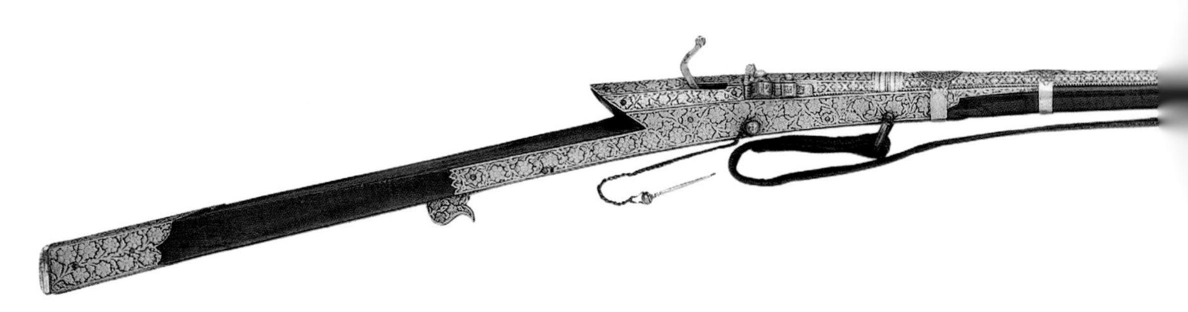

▲ Matchlock musket (*toradar*)

Decorated with gold *koftgari*, with vent pricker attached. From the Indian disarmament of 1859, presented by the Indian government, 1861. XXVIF.127

► Belt with powder flask and pouches for bullets (*kamr*)

This seems to match the record from the Toshakhana inventory for a *kamr* that was commissioned by Maharaja Ranjit Singh for the wedding of his son Kharak Singh in 1838. XXVIF.38

the East India Company and sent back to England for display at the Tower. When it arrived, the gift comprised of nearly 200 pieces of arms and armour from all over India, their provenances carefully recorded as well as the names by which they were known.
This formed the first study of the names of Indian weapons in the West, and set the standard for all subsequent nomenclature of Indian arms when it was published as part of the catalogue by John Hewitt in 1859. Recent research into the gift has suggested that possible links can be drawn between some of the gift items and objects which were listed in Dr John Login's inventory of the Sikh treasury (*Toshakhana*) in Lahore as having direct connections to important Sikh leaders, including Maharaja Ranjit Singh himself.

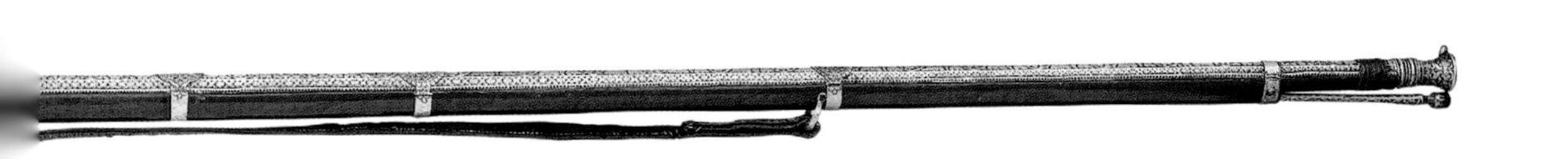

▶ Water-colour illustration of *The Indian Court and Elephant Trappings*, The Great Exhibition of 1851, Crystal Palace, Hyde Park, by Goodall.

The Great Exhibition

At around the same time as the East India Company gift, another substantial acquisition was made following the Great Exhibition of 1851. The contents of the 'Indian Court' were distributed in 1852, and the Armouries purchased over 100 pieces of arms and armour. The majority were practical objects, but some were interesting curiosities, such as the pistol shield and the *khanda* with accompanying *katar* and pistol which have been featured on previous pages of this book. These weapons were produced to show high levels of skill and craftsmanship to impress exhibition-goers.

Indian disarmament, 1859

After the Indian Mutiny, the British government assumed direct rule over India and took measures to improve the effectiveness and security of its control. The ratio of European to native troops in the Indian army was increased, and an act was passed in 1859 to permanently disarm the local Indian population. Magistrates were permitted to enter homes in search of illegal arms; if unlicensed weapons were discovered they were confiscated and the owner subjected to imprisonment or corporal punishment. The government ended up with a cache of contraband weaponry as a result, and in 1861 the Tower Armouries was presented with over 100 items which had been amassed during the disarmament.

The Codrington collection

The East India Company gift contained a substantial group of pieces associated with Tipu Sultan of Mysore, but purchase of the Codrington collection in 1863 added substantially to this. Codrington had been an officer of Native Infantry in Madras, and had built up a considerable collection. The Tower bought extensively from the sale, and divided the haul between their own collection and that of the Rotunda Museum of the Regiment of Artillery at Woolwich. The Woolwich section is sadly now dispersed.

The Tower collection

The Tower collection, built up with care in the 19th century was transferred to the British Museum in 1914 under the Master of the Armouries Charles ffoulkes, who felt non-European arms and armour inappropriate to the Tower of London. The collection was largely recovered by Russell Robinson, Keeper of Armour from 1945–78, who re-established the Oriental Gallery at the Tower, first on the ground floor of the New Armouries (at the time of writing a restaurant) and in 1975, on the ground floor of the Waterloo Building (whence it was removed in 1991 to make way for the new display of the Crown Jewels). In 1996 the collection was redisplayed in its largest and grandest form to date in the new Oriental Gallery in the Royal Armouries Museum in Leeds.

◄ View of the Oriental Gallery at Leeds.

SIKH WARRIOR

A complete set of equipment for a Sikh warrior of the early 19th century, with armour of butted mail, plate cuirass, helmet, arm defences and shield, together with a matchlock musket and set of firearms accoutrements of a specially designed belt, and sword with its scabbard and baldrick. This composite equipment records many of the different phases of acquisition of the Royal Armouries' Indian collection. The armour and musket were acquired before 1859, the sword formed part of the gift of Asian arms and armour given to the Tower Armouries in 1853 by the Honourable East India Company, the shield was probably given as a diplomatic gift to Prince Alfred, second son of Queen Victoria during his visit to India in 1869–70, and given by Her Majesty the Queen to the Tower Armouries in 1954, and the firearms accoutrements were purchased from the Great Exhibition of 1851. XXVIA.8, 22, XXVIF.119, 136, XXVIS.138

GLOSSARY

The terminology of Indian arms and armour is difficult, partly because of the fact that a given weapon could be quite correctly called by different names by speakers of different languages. The names of some of the more standard types, together with their language of origin in standard transliteration, are given below.

ankus	elephant goad (Hindi)
ayudha katti	'war' sword (Tamil)
bagh nakh	tiger claw (Hindi)
ballam	spear (Hindi)
barcha	all-steel spear (Hindi ?)
bargustavan	horse armour (Persian)
bargustavan -i-pil	elephant armour (Persian)
bazuband	arm defence (Persian)
bhuj	elephant-bladed axe (Gujarat)
bichwa	'scorpian' dagger (Hindi)
bullova	axe, Kol
bunga dastar	Akali turban (Panjabi)
chahar a'ineh	'four mirrors', plate body armour (Persian)
chakra	throwing quoit (Hindi)
changal	swivel gun (Persian)
chihal'ta hazar masha	coat of 1,000 nails (Persian)
chura	Afghan 'Khyber knife' (Pashto)
cumberjung	double flail (Gujarati)
dao	sword or chopper, Assam (Chinese)
dastana	arm defence (Hindi)
deg	bronze mortar, Mysore
dhal	shield (Hindi)
dhunook	self-bow, Chota Nagpur
firanghi	European ('foreign')-bladed sword (Persian)
gardani	neck defence for a horse (crinet) (Persian)
gorz	mace (Persian)
jaza'il	matchlock musket (Persian)
joshan	body armour generally (Arabic)
jouhar	lustre of watered steel
kajim	body armour for a horse (peytral, flanchard and crupper) (Persian)
kaman	composite bow
kamr	belt, for sword or firearms accoutrements (Persian)
kard	knife (Persian)
katar	punch dagger (Hindi)
katariya	throwing stick, south India
khanda	straight sword (Hindi)
koftgari	overlaid decoration (Persian)
khanjar	curved bladed dagger (Persian, Arabic)
kolah khod	plate helmet (Persian)
kolah zereh	mail and plate helmet (Persian)
madu	parrying weapon, south India
migfer	helmet (Turkish)
nezah	lance (Persian)
pajama zirah	armoured trousers (Hindi, Persian)
pandi ballam	hog hunting spear (Hindi)
pata	gauntlet sword (Hindi)
pazipent	arm defence (Turkish)
peti	armour (Hindi)
pharetra	axe used by Khonds (Khond)
pichangatti	knife (Tamil)
pulouar	curved sword (Afghan)
pushqabz	single edged dagger (Persian)
qashqah	head defence for a horse (shaffron) (Persian)
ratha	war chariot (Sanskrit)
sangin	bayonet
separ	shield (Persian)
shamshir	curved sword (Persian)
shast	archer's thumb ring (Persian)
sosun pata	forward curved ('lily') sword (Hindi)
tabarzin	saddle axe (Persian)

talwar	curved sword (Hindi)	*zaghnol*	'crow bill', a type of axe (Persian)
tir	arrow (Persian)	*zamburak*	camel gun (literally 'wasp') (Persian)
tongi	axe (Khond) (Hindi)	*zehgir*	archer's thumb ring (Persian)
tup	cannon (Turkish)	*zel*	bowstring (Persian)
top	helmet (Hindi)	*zereh*	mail armour (Persian)
toradar	matchlock musket (Hindi)	*zereh bagtar*	mail and plate armour (Persian)
vercheroval	sickle-shaped weapon, Coorg		

FURTHER READING

Alexander, D 1992 *The arts of war: arms and armour of the 7th to 19th centuries. The Nasser D. Khalili Collection of Islamic Art.* London, Nour Foundation (UK) Limited in association with Azimuth Editions and Oxford University Press

Egerton, W 1880 *An illustrated handbook of Indian arms*, London, W H Allen (2nd edition of 1895 includes an appendix on Egerton's own collection, bequeathed in 1910 to the Manchester City Art Gallery, reprinted Bangkok, White Orchid Press, 1981)

Elgood, R (ed.) 1979 *Islamic arms and armour.* London, Scolar Press

Elgood, R 1995 *Firearms of the Islamic world in the Tareq Rajab Museum, Kuwait.* London, I.B. Taurus

Elgood, R 2005 *Hindu arms and ritual.* Delft, Eburon

Haider, S Z 1991 *Islamic arms and armour of northdern India.* Lahore, Badahur

Hales, R 2013 *Islamic and Oriental arms and armour: a lifetime's passion.* Robert Hales C.I. Ltd

Mohamed, B 2008 *The arts of the Muslim knight: The Furusiyya Art Foundation Collection.* Milan, Skira Editore

Pant, G N and **K K Sharma** 2001 *Indian armours in the National Museum collection.* New Delhi

Pant, G N 1997 *Horse and elephant armour.* New Dehli, Agam Kala Prakasham

Rawson, P S 1968 *The Indian sword.* London, Herbert Jenkins

Ricketts, H and **Missillier, P** 1988 *Splendeur des armes orientales.* Paris, Acte-Expo

Robinson, H R 1967 *Oriental Armour.* London, Herbert Jenkins Ltd

Stone, G C 1934 *A glossary of the construction, decoration and use of armor and arms.* Portland, Massachusetts, (includes much of Stone's own collection, bequeathed to the Metropolitan Museum of Art, New York)

Stronge, S 1999 *The arts of the Sikh kingdoms.* London, V&A

The right of Thom Richardson and Natasha Bennett to be identified as the authors of this work has been asserted in accordance with the Copyright Designs and Patents Act 1988.

Series Editor: Debbie Wurr
Series Designer: Geraldine Mead
Series Photographers: Gary Ombler, Rod Joyce

Royal Armouries Museum, Armouries Drive, Leeds LS10 1LT

First published 2007

ISBN 978-0-948092-74-9

Printed in Singapore